DUNKIRK

A Miracle of Deliverance

By the Same author

The Bottomless Pit

DUNKIRK —

A Miracle of Deliverance

by

Frederick Grossmith

Bachman & Turner Ltd
London

First published 1979
by
Bachman & Turner Ltd
The Old Hop Exchange
1/3 Central Buildings
Southwark Street
London SE1

ISBN 0 85974 078 1

Typeset by Inforum Ltd, Portsmouth
Printed in Great Britain by offset
lithography & also bound by
Billing & Sons Ltd, Guildford,
London and Worcester.

CONTENTS

LIST OF ILLUSTRATIONS

Page

ACKNOWLEDGEMENTS

In sending this book out to the public I should like to make certain ackowledgements.

Firstly, an expression of sincere thanks and appreciation to Vilma Gardner, Linda Aberdeen and Lynn Wilson for their patient and excellent work in preparing the typescript.

Also to the editors of the following newspapers and magazines for their kindness in allowing me to reprint previously published items and reproduce their photographic work in this book. In addition some were most helpful to me during the days of research.

A sincere thank you to:

The New York Times; Northampton Chronicle and Echo; The Daily Telegraph and C.B. Mortlock; The Grimsby Evening Telegraph; The Manchester Evening News; Journal of The Dunkirk Veterans Association; Mr. Harold Stough and The National Message; Isle of Man Steam Packet Company Limited; Billy Tidy; Malcom Mills.

I have a deep debt of gratitude to the many Dunkirk Veterans who took the trouble to write me with such wonderful personalised stories and without whose help this book could not have been written.

If unwittingly I have made some ommission I trust any such oversight will be forgiven.

FRED GROSSMITH

*So long as the English Tongue survives, the word
Dunkirk will be spoken with reverence.*

NEW YORK TIMES
June 1st, 1940

This book is dedicated to the members of the Dunkirk
Veterans Association who against all odds wrote a page
of British history that should be inscribed in letters of
gold.

WITH GOD'S HELP WE SHALL PREVAIL

"The task will be hard. There may be dark days ahead
... but we can only do the right as we see the right, and
reverently commit our cause to God. If one and all we
keep resolutely faithful to it, ready for whatever Service
and Sacrifice it may demand, then with God's help, we
shall prevail."

HIS MAJESTY KING GEORGE VI
IN A BROADCAST TO THE NATION
ON THE EVENING OF SEPT. 3RD, 1939
FROM BUCKINGHAM PALACE.

"I shall always count it a privilege to have been at Dunkirk and to
have belonged afterwards to the admirable Dunkirk Veterans'
Association, who have done so much to keep going that spirit of
comradeship and endeavour which was so much in evidence in
those stirring times."

BRIGADIER SIR JOHN SMITH, BT., V.C., M.C.

The Author, Minister of Calvary Church, Grimsby and Chaplain to the area D.V.A. Branch, receiving a plaque to be placed in the 'Dunkirk' memorial corner of the Church.

CHAPTER ONE

'The German Has Come Back'

On May, 10th, 1940 for the second time in 26 years, Germany violated the neutrality of Belgium. A special edition of *La Nation Belgie* was headlined 'The German Has Come Back'. Hearts sank. The toll of the Great War had mangled Belgium, robbing countless homes of loved ones and producing battle sites which had become household names. This then was one war they not only wished to be free from but had actually believed would not trouble their beloved soil.

To Hitler, all laws of morality, codes of ethics, treaties, were discretionary and subject to change. He was no respector of persons. So much so that even before Herr von Buelow-Schwante, Hitler's Ambassador in Brussels called upon M. Spaak, Belgian Foreign Minister, Brussels, Antwerp and other cities had been raided by German bombers. One newspaper reporter wired, 'The People Stared, Amazed', as shortly after 5 a.m. German planes appeared over Brussels. The imaginary curtains veiling a false security, were drawn back. The Belgian Government issued a general mobilisation proclamation and appealed to Britain and France for aid, King Leopold taking charge of military operations.

On that same Black Friday, of May, 10th, neighbouring Holland was invaded when at 2.40 a.m. German bombers appeared over Amsterdam. Airfields and most vital centres of communication were attacked; Amsterdam was bombed. Troop-carrying planes deposited their deadly cargo in the skies of Holland, the first parachutists arriving soon after 4 a.m. Through perfect planning, the Hague and many important centres were encircled. During the day, parachutists descended in various parts of the country, attacking airports, military barracks and generally hitting where it hurt most of all. To make matters all the more difficult, reports began to filter through to the effect that the sky invaders did not always appear to be wearing German uniforms. Some were landing dressed as Dutch or British Soldiers. Others as petticoated country girls and even Dutch parsons. Dutch defences were penetrated by conventional and unconventional methods.

In a proclamation to the Dutch people, Queen Wilhelmina said:—

> After our country, with scrupulous conscientiousness, had observed strict neutrality during all these months, and while Holland had no other plan than to maintain this attitude, Germany last night made a sudden attack on our territory without warning. This was done notwithstanding the solemn promise that the neutrality of our country would be respected as long as we ourselves maintained that neutrality.
> I herewith make a flaming protest against this unprecedented violation of good faith and violation of all that is decent between cultured States. I and my Government will also do our duty now. Do your duty everywhere and in all circumstances. Everyone to the post to which he is appointed, with the utmost vigilance and with that inner calmness and strongheartedness which a clear conscience gives.

Naturally, Hitler had a ready answer. In a radio broadcast from Berlin to announce the invasion of Belgium and Holland, spokesman Goebbels claimed Belgium had since the beginning of the war undertaken a military build-up despite her official neutrality. He felt they cleaved to a one sided policy in their demonstration of heavily fortifying the Eastern Frontier but not her Frontier with France. As for the Dutch, the pattern was similar in their coastal regions. Plus the fact of permitting British aircraft, daily to fly over Holland. Goebbels accused both nations of aiding the British Secret Service in planning a revolution in Germany. "Worked out on Dutch Soil", he stated, the plan, "was to overthrow the Fuehrer and the German Government and establish another Government which would agree on the annihilation of the Reich and the creation of a series of federal states". In consequence, the Reich Government gave an order to German troops, "to safeguard the neutrality of these countries by all means".

The unduly schismatic Hitler, suffering from acute megalomania, saw himself as a man of destiny. Like all megalomaniacs he had a mania for big things. He believed the Third Reich had an overwhelming dynamic of power which would sweep Europe like an irresistible whirlwind.

At times he underwent bouts of melancholia, being completely unapproachable when in such depressive condition. On May 10th, 1940, however, he could be designated a monomaniac; totally obsessed with one single subject, namely to smash down all resistance by demonstrating the superiority of the German. He would out-gun and out-wit every allied endeavour. To prove he was a military genius, he allowed his thrust into Belgium and Holland to have every appearance of the famous Schlieffen Plan of 1914 with an enveloping sweep on the right flank. In 1914 the German commander-in-Chief, Von Moltke, adhering to this plan, lost his nerve and refused to take in Holland in his drive to the West. German analysts have always declared it was a costly error which lost them the war. Hitler not only rectified the situation by including Holland — he flavoured it with the genius of deception. "I succeeded", he said, "in deceiving the enemy staffs by inverting the Schlieffen Plan". The original plan necessitated a thrust through the northern districts of Belgium past Antwerp and Ghent to the Channel Ports of France. Hitler, arranged for operations to bear mainly on the left wing of the front. "It was made easier", he said, "by the enemy himself, who had concentrated all his motorised troops on the Belgian Frontier. I attacked the right flank and succeeded".

In addition to the attacks on Belgium and Holland, on the same day Germany presented a memorandum to Luxemburg to the effect that in order for an Allied attack to be counteracted German military operations will cover Luxemburg as well. Hitler viewed the mighty Maginot Line, which some designated as being 'impregnable', as a challenge. This huge mass of fortification stretched across the whole French — German border. Its vast bastion of steel and concrete presented a most formidable defence. The French claimed the Maginot Line could never be taken by frontal assault. Rather than allowing experience furnish an answer, Hitler was prepared to take them at their word. Although the Maginot Line could be catalogued as stretching across the French — German border, there was some exception. The Ardennes Forest had no defensive concrete and Hitler viewed this as a chink in the armour. The architects of the Maginot Line considered the Ardennes as impassable. The hilly terrain of Luxemburg with its dense woods provided a natural barrier of defence. Certainly no German army could attack through the forest. The Reich military strategists shared such views. Not so, however, by Hitler. Alarm spread amongst his generals when he insisted the forest approach revealed the only way to outflank. Naturally, he had his own way. Whilst the eyes and ears of the world were held by the events in Belgium and Holland, at 3 a.m. on that same morning of May 10th, 1940, divisions plus tanks moved into the Ardennes. A brilliant move and one that the Allied H.Q. knew nothing about until 15 hours later.

Meanwhile, another battle took place on May 10th. This time in Britain. At 8 a.m. that morning the War Cabinet met at No. 10 Downing Street. The meeting lasted 35 minutes. Afterwards, Mr. Churchill, then First Lord of the Admiralty, told reporters, "I think you will understand that plenty happened last night, and something is happening today". Criticism of the Government had been mounting. The learned gentlemen who during the 'thirties' had peddled the doctrine of 'appeasement', whilst remaining garrulous seemed in a fuddle. The complacent attitude adopted by the Government with regard to the conduct of the war brought rumblings of dissatisfaction from every corner of the nation. The time had come for 'heads to roll'. At 6 p.m. Prime Minister Neville Chamberlain handed his resignation to the King, who immediately called upon Winston Churchill to form a new Government. Later in the evening Mr. Chamberlain broadcast to the nation the news of his resignation:—

> Early this morning, without warning or excuse, Hitler added another to the horrible crimes which already disgrace his name by a sudden attack on Holland, Belgium and Luxemburg. In all history no other man has been responsible for such a hideous toll of human suffering and misery as he.
>
> He has chosen a moment when perhaps it seemed to him that this country was entangled in the throes of a political crisis and when he might find it divided against itself. If he has counted on our internal divisions to help him he has miscalculated the minds of this people.
>
> I am not now going to make any comment on the debate of the House of Commons which took place on Tuesday and Wednesday, but when it was over I had no doubt in my mind that some new and drastic action must be taken if condifence was to be restored in the House of Commons and the war carried on with the vigour and energy essential to victory.
>
> It was clear that at this critical moment in the war what was needed was the formation of a Government which would include members of the Liberal and Labour Opposition, and thus present a united front to the enemy.
>
> By this afternoon it was apparant that the essential unity could be secured under another Prime Minister. In these circumstances my duty was plain. I sought an audience of the King this evening and tendered to him my resignation which His Majesty has been pleased to accept.
>
> The King has now entrusted to my friend and colleague Mr. Winston Churchill, the task of forming a new Administration on a national basis, and in this task I have no doubt he will be successful. . . .

Churchill undertook the task of forming his Coalition Government. Later that night the appointment of a War Cabinet was announced, namely:—

> The Prime Minister
> Mr. N. Chamberlain — Lord President of the Council
> Mr. C. Atlee — Leader of the Labour Party
> Lord Halifax — Foreign Secretary
> Mr. A. Greenwood — Deputy Leader of the Labour Party.

On the 11th May, the Service Ministers, were announced:—

Mr. A. Eden — Minister for War (Conservative)
Mr. A. Alexander — First Lord of the Admiralty (Labour)
Sir A. Sinclair — Secretary for Air (Liberal)

The Service Ministers were not members of the War Cabinet. Churchill himself was to be Minister of Defence.

On following days, other appointments were made:

Herbert Morrison as Minister of Supply
Ernest Bevin as Minister of Labour
Duff Cooper as Minister of Information
Lord Woolton as Minister of Food
Lord Beaverbrook as Minister of Aircraft Production
Sir Kingsley Wood as Chancellor of the Exchequer
Sir John Simon as Lord Chancellor
Sir John Anderson as Home Secretary

Grave responsibilities rested upon the shoulders of Britain's new leader and his team. Immediately the Government moved into action. The decisive implementation of policies long called for by Press and public, were soon furnished.

Britain's new leaders awoke the nation from its nine month 'nap'. Alert to the fact that in order to fight a war, guns, tanks, planes, ships and ammunition were a necessity. Production needed to be speeded up. Provided, of course, Hitler didn't beat us to it by paying a personal visit. Hence, a clear policy of home defence had to be initiated. Within a week the formation of the 'Local Defence Volunteers' was announced, later to be designated, 'Home Guard'. Today, known with affection as 'Dad's Army'. On one day alone, 250,000 applied to join. It was a race against time.

British history records the unsuccessful attempts of would-be invaders, and for over 900 years Great Britain has remained unconquerable. When the critical and crucial hour has struck — might men of valour and wisdom have appeared, as if born for that very hour.

Britain will never know how much it owed to Winston Churchill. At 65 years of age and having spend many years in the political 'doldrums' some thought he was ripe to put out to 'grass'. None could escape the fact of the reality of his prophecies. For years, this life-long student of war had warned of such an hour coming upon the nation. Following his appointment with the King from which he returned home as Prime Minister, he said:—

I felt as if I were walking with destiny, and that all my past life had been but a preparation for this hour and for this trial.

If Hitler had thought he would take advantage of the British domestic situation, in the early hours of May 10th, he must have felt quite smug with himself, as he rained his flagitious attack upon Belgium, Holland and Luxemburg. However, before that day was through the smile would perhaps have disappeared and a less complacent Hitler would have emerged. Churchill, was one Englishman he seemed to fear. His speeches referred to Churchill more frequently than Prime Minister Chamberlain. Even before the outbreak of hostilities, Hitler made references to Churchill.

October 1938
"I am fully aware that if one day the place of Chamberlain were taken by such men as Eden, Duff Cooper or Churchill, their aim would be to unleash at once a new world war against Germany".

November 1938
"After all, Churchill may have 14,000, 20,000 or 30,000 votes behind him — I am not so well informed about that — but I have 40,000,000 behind me".

In January, 1933 Hitler became Chancellor of Germany. From that time, British politicians had viewed him from many sides. Various opinions were expressed. Always, the voice of Churchill spelt out in no uncertain terms a warning of 'the German Menace'. He ridiculed the Government's ineffectual approach to the nation's defence Programme, Hitler was a threat.

Catalogued, 'a warmonger', Churchill experienced an isolation, hitherto unknown to himself: save for a few like-minded visionaries who continued to raise their voices; demanding action to meet the developing threat of Hitler — it was not fashionable to be found in the company of Winston Churchill. In these years of 'isolation', he spend much time at home. It enabled him to work upon his biography of his ancestor, Marlborough.

Consequent upon the Abdication Crisis of King Edward VIII Prime Minister Baldwin resigned. May, 1937 found Britain with a new Premier. Neville Chamberlain overlooked Churchill when forming his Cabinet. Some were of the opinion he feared Churchill would relegate him to being 'captain of the ship' in name only.

When Chamberlain returned from Munich after adding his signature to the Munich Agreement, Churchill spoke out. 'Peace in our time', appeared all the more an aphorism of absurdity. Duff Cooper, who felt as Churchill did, resigned as First Lord of the Admiralty. The time was September, 1938.

Throughout 1939, ominous signs caused the British press to proclaim the name of Churchill. Thinking men viewed the Munich Agreement as nothing more than a 'scrap of paper'. Chamberlain's 'peace in our time', was not the 'lullaby of security' it at first appeared to be. Churchill was on the way back.

At 11 a.m. on Sunday, September 3rd, 1939, Britain entered into hostilities with Hitler's Germany. The man who for so long had prophesied that such an event would come to pass received an invitation to join the Cabinet in the capacity of First Lord of the Admiralty. Churchill was back.

On May, 13th, 1940, Winston Churchill made his first speech as Prime Minister in the House of Commons:—

> I would say to the House as I said to those who have joined this Government: "I have nothing to offer but blood, toil, tears and sweat". We have before us an ordeal of the most grievous kind. We have before us many, many long months of struggle and of suffering. You ask what is our policy; I will say: It is to wage war, by sea, land and air, with all our might and with all the strength that God can give us, and to wage war against a monstrous tyranny, never surpassed in the dark, lamentable catalogue of human crime. That is our policy.
>
> You ask what is our aim; I can answer in one word. It is victory — victory at all costs — victory in spite of all terrors — victory, however long and hard the road may be; for without victory there is no survival — let that be realised — no survival for the British Empire, no survival for all that the British Empire has stood for, no survival for the urge and impulse of the ages, that mankind will move forward towards its goal.
>
> I take up my task with buoyancy and hope, and I feel sure that our cause will not be suffered to fail among men. At this time I feel entitled to claim the aid of all, and I say: Come then, let us go forward together with our united strength.

Truly a message that gave confidence and hope. The forerunner of many mighty speeches. Six days later, Churchill gave his first broadcast as head of the Government. He closed by saying:—

> Today is Trinity Sunday. Centuries ago words were written to be a call and a spur to faithful servants of truth and justice: "Arm yourselves, and be Ye men of valour, and be in readiness for the conflict, for it is better for us to perish in battle than to look on the outrage of our nation and our altars. As the will of God is in Heaven, even so let Him do".

May, 10th, 1940 when it was written "The German Has Come Back" also signalled the day 'Churchill has Come Back', to lead a united Britain, determined to fight on; if necessary alone.

Well, your danger is as you have seen. And truly I am sorry it is so great, but I would have it cause no despondency, as truly I think it will not, for we are Englishmen.

OLIVER CROMWELL

CHAPTER TWO

Holland and Belgium

HOLLAND

Despite the valiant efforts of the Dutch military forces, there was no answer to the complete air superiority of the Luftwaffe. Concern for strict neutrality had naturally hindered the co-ordination of plans with allied neighbours against the day when Holland would have to resist German aggression.

As already mentioned, Hitler did not intend to test the French boast regarding the Maginot Line. He anticipated the action the Allied forces would take should it appear he was following the Schlieffen Plan of 1914. He therefore decided to launch the assault in the north against lightly defended Holland. The Dutch nation, meticulous in its endeavour to demonstrate an honest appearance of neutrality, would not take long to overrun. A speedy occupation of Holland was vital in order to secure the northern flank.

Using mainly paratroops and glider-borne forces, the German attack was made by the 7th Airborne Division and by 22nd Infantry Division. The task of the 22nd Division, an army airborne division focussed upon the Hague. Three aerodromes near the Hague-Valkenburg, Ockenburg and Ypenburg were soon in German hands. This enabled their transport planes, filled with troops to land, the plan being to capture the Hague on the first day of the campaign. Confidence was high and Lieutenant-General Graf von Sponeck the commander of the airborne forces could be seen arrayed in full-dress uniform. The Hague, where were the Royal Court and seat of Government, was encircled by his forces. Soon he expected an audience with Queen Wilhelmina and resultant submission of Dutch forces.

From the air, leaflets dropped on the town explained the hopeless position and urged surrender. But the Bible says, "Wherefore let him that thinketh he standeth take heed lest he fall" 1 CORINTHIANS 10 v.12, and by nightfall, Von Sponeck had fallen. The airfields taken earlier in the day were littered with the wreckage of German aircraft.

The dead were many, but it was not some secret mighty army that had done all this damage. Merely, the small Dutch Air Force

18

together with Dutch troops who in the majority of cases could boast of one month's service — troops whom the German High Command had designated as 'worthless and undisciplined'. Their determined efforts secured the safety of Queen Wilhelmina and her Government.

Meanwhile, the 7th Airborne Division, a Luftwaffe unit had successfully seized Waalhaven Airport and occupied on area of the city of Rotterdam. Throughout the day heavy reinforcements streamed into the airport. Dutch counter attacks at ground and air level were heroic but costly. The Germans fully realised they would encounter some difficulty in facing Holland's natural barrier — water. The large estuaries of the Rivers Maas and Rhine give Holland its own water line and to the invader, water was a serious obstacle. The four main crossing points; the great Moerdijk bridge spanning the chief estuary of the River Maas, known as the Hollandock Diep which separates North and South Holland; Dordrecht and the bridges in the centre of Rotterdam, became important military objectives. On May 13th German armoured columns crossed the Moerdijk bridge and its capture signalled the futility of further resistance. The Germans were in a hurry to wrap the whole job up. In the evening of May 13th, General Rudolf Schmidt called on the Dutch commander, Colonel Scharoo, to surrender. This was ignored. Late next morning an ultimatum was delivered — surrender or the Luftwaffe would destroy the city centre. The Colonel contacted The Hague and within the hour a reply was received to the effect that a delegation would be sent to Rotterdam to discuss terms of surrender. General Schmidt sent a signal for the attack to be called off. He was too late. That afternoon two square miles of central Rotterdam were laid waste in the short time of thirty minutes. 100 Heinkel bombers attacked the city converting it into a veritable heap of rubbish. Some 25,000 houses were razed making 80,000 people homeless. Even now there is a mystery as to the actual number of persons killed during the "horror raid". At first figures of 30-35,000 were quoted. Today, the Dutch speak in terms of around 1,000 persons.

Surrender! It seemed a sad thought but inevitable. So deliberated General H.G. Winkleman, Commander-in-Chief of the Netherlands Sea and Land Forces. His forces had lost nearly 5,000 men killed and wounded. It appeared the asault on Rotterdam was a sample of what the Luftwaffe would mete out to other towns and cities. So at half-past nine next morning he signed the document of surrender. His mood is summed up in a broadcast made to the nation:

> We have laid down our arms because we must. We had decided to defend our Fatherland to the very limit. Today we have reached that limit. Our soldiers have fought with the courage

which will always be beyond compare. In face of the technical methods of the enemy this was not enough. In thousands they have fallen in defence of the liberty of the Netherlands. Our Air Forces were so reduced that they could no longer support the army. We could not fight against the German superiority in the air. And among the civilian population also numerous victims have fallen in the air raids. Rotterdam has undergone the sad experience of total war. Utrecht and other cities were threatened the same way. These facts have led me to this very serious decision. We have given up fighting... Long live her Majesty the Queen! Long live the Fatherland!

Meanwhile, Princess Juliana, with Prince Bernhard and their two children had reached England aboard the British destroyer *Codrington*. Queen Wilhelmina had intended to leave for Zeeland aboard a British warship. However, due to heavy enemy bombardment the destroyer made for an English port. Later the same day members of the Dutch Government followed the Queen to England.

After an engagement of a mere five days Holland had been overthrown. But Holland was still at war. In a proclamation to the Dutch people, Queen Wilhelmina made her feelings very clear, 'The Government are now in England. They are not prepared, as a Government, to capitulate. Consequently, the territory of the Netherlands remaining in our hands, in Europe as well as in the East and West Indies, continues to be a sovereign State, able to assert its place as a full member of the community of States, and in particular in the joint deliberations of the Allies'.

BELGIUM

The airborne thrusts of the offensive made the Belgian Army aware that the sky belonged to Hitler. This was exactly the reputation Hitler wished to earn. Belgian hopes rested in their careful planning to defend their beloved soil. Along the Albert Canal, stretching from Antwerp to Liege heavy fortifications were in evidence. Situated on the canal, the huge fort of Eben Emael provided its own deterrent to any would-be attacker; the Belgians considered the Fort almost impregnable. For some time Hitler had been considering the situation. He was sensitive to history and realised the Albert Canal defences plus those along the River Meuse, from Liege to Namur, were to fulfil a special place by buying time for the French and British. In 1914 the Belgians had undertaken a similar project and escaped. The Kaiser's armies met bitter opposition with tremendous losses and progress was slow. Hitler now trod that same road and he intended to display to all he was the conqueror of conquerors.

The scheme to capture the two bridges over the Albert Canal and the Fort of Eben Emael took root in the mind of Hitler. He needed those bridges intact and in his heated imagination he had a most beautiful vision of a dark night and silently his troops descending, through the night sky, upon their objectives. In reality, his parachute troops proved to be most effective. Now for the Fort he would show to his enemies a movement of daring novelty and surprise. Gliders were not exactly the craze of the hour, in fact they were the most unlikely aircraft to be found in the combatant skies of 1940. Eleven gliders landed on the top of Fort Eben Emael and brilliantly set into motion a much rehearsed plan to render the Fort completely inert. Armed with two tons of explosives they destroyed the armament, kept the strong garrison of troops in check whilst tanks crashed over the outer pill-boxes and ground troops arrived to secure the position.

Over the captured Albert Canal bridges streamed the might of German armoured and mechanised forces. The Belgians withdrew to the main defensive positions on the Antwerp-Namur line. By May 17th Brussels was in German hands, the Belgian Government having set up office in Ostend. Hitler and his Generals were eager for speedy conquest and as they studied their maps, carefully plotting every Allied withdrawal, they became elated. Successes in France and the anticipated action of the French and British in weakening their positions along the French frontier in order to add strength to the Belgian campaign, now gave Hitler the opportunity he had long awaited. To open a corridor between the Allied armies in Belgium and their main forces, south of the Somme in France, would put the German right within sight of total victory.

The seriousness of the situation was summed up in an 'Order of the Day' issued by the Allied Supreme Commander — General Maurice Gamelin:—

> The fate of our country and that of our Allies, the destinies of the World, depend on the battle now in progress. British, Belgian, Polish soldiers and foreign volunteers are fighting at our side, and the Royal Air Force is taking its full part with our own. Any soldier who cannot advance should allow himself to be killed rather than abandon that part of our national soil which has been entrusted to him. As always in grave hours of our history, the Order of the Day is 'Conquer or Die'. We must conquer.

The message was received in the spirit that it had been given. The French Government decided a change of leadership was needed and forty eight hours later, Gamelin was 'sacked' and succeeded by General Weygand. It was now Sunday, May 19th.

CHAPTER THREE

Boulogne and Calais

BOULOGNE

Situated 20 miles south west of Calais Boulogne is a busy port having a natural harbour, and during World War I it served as the main British Army base.

In AD 82 it was occupied by the Romans who named it Portus Gesoriacus. Later the name was changed to Bononis. In 1430 the Duke of Burgandy took over which led to rule under French Monarchy during the reign of Louis XI in 1477. Another change of ownership took place in 1544 when it came into the hands of England's Henry VIII but six years later he sold out to Charles IX. In 1803, Napoleon Bonaparte gathered 180,000 men and 2,400 ships there with the intention of invading England. He anticipated the sweet taste of victory — England would crown all his conquests. He said:—

> Let us be masters of the channel for six hours and we are masters of the World. . . The English do not know what is hanging over them if we can be masters of the channel . . . England will have ceased to be.

Later, we shall see that Napoleon was not first in the field to exercise optimism of a successful invasion of England only to find the forces of nature working against him.

The success of the German breakthrough to the coast at Abbeville on May 20th gave Boulogne a new significance. Together with Calais and Dunkirk they were the only ports through which the British Expeditionary Force could be supplied.

Unlike World War I days no British garrison had been stationed there. The British Expeditionary Force, now fighting for its life could do nothing about its defence. There was a strong possibility that the Germans might enter the port without opposition.

On the morning of May 21st, two battalions of the 20th Guards Brigade were ordered from Camberley to Dover for overseas service. Within twenty-four hours, under the command of Brigadier Fox-Pitt, they were in Boulogne. During the previous day anti-aircraft defences had been provided with two troops of the 2nd Heavy

Anti-Aircraft Regiment providing eight 3.7 inch guns and two Troops of the 58th Light Anti-Aircraft Regiment setting up eight machine guns. One battery of the 2nd Searchlight Regiment completed the British armament.

But Boulogne had other visitors. Streams of frightened refugees made their hurried appearance in the seaport town. Mingling with them were many French and Belgian troops, some in a state of exhaustion, the fruits of the havoc caused by the speedy advance of the enemy. In addition, several hundred British soldiers, survivors of the 36th Brigade had reached the town.

By far the largest body of men to arrive *en bloc*, comprised some 1500 Pioneer Corps. Known as 'chunkies', they belonged to the baby corps of the British Army. They were the army's labour force and completely untrained for the immediate task of defending the town. They had arrived at Wimereux, about three miles up the coast. Wimereux had now taken on a new importance, serving as Rear General Headquarters of the B.E.F. However, the Commanding Officer, Lieutenant Colonel Dean, knew what war was all about, having in World War I won the Victoria Cross. To his drive and initiative, the Pioneer Corps owed their safe retreat.

The defence of Boulogne fell upon Brigadier Fox-Pitt. Simply, he was ordered to hold the town, with the promise that tanks and infantry would be sent to him from Calais. Naturally, such news brought a sigh of relief. Unknown to the Brigadier, Calais had its own serious problems and history reveals the promise was not fulfilled.

Immediately, plans for the defence of the town were implemented.

Boulogne is surrounded by hills. It is through a valley in these hills that the River Liane makes its way to the sea. The arrangement of the harbour basins together with the river, slices the lower town into two halves. Only in the harbour area is the ground flat. Facing the harbour lies the shopping area and instantly a complete change is noticeable as all roads up are very steep. I realised just how steep when carrying a heavy suitcase from the port on my way to Boulogne-Ville Railway Station. At the top stands the old walled town.

Whoever commanded the heights of Boulogne — commanded Boulogne. The French held a fort at Ville Haute situated in the old walled-in area of the town which looked down upon the harbour. Brigadier Fox-Pitt wisely deployed his meagre force of resistance but once the enemy located his defence the position could not be maintained.

The withdrawal was magnificent. Against tanks and superior numbers much heroism was demonstrated. Some of the Pioneer Corps had been transferred from Wimereux to act as dock labourers. Others to hold road block positions. Only about 400 Pioneers had been issued with rifles. Far less than this number knew what to do with them. One group of Pioneers, 'Gentlemen from Scotland', came face to face with some enemy infantry. They discarded their rifles and attacked the enemy with long-bladed razors. And overcame them.

In the sky, the Royal Air Force played a vital role in an endeavour to slow down the German advance upon the town, inflicting much damage to the enemy for few losses.

The Royal Navy from harbour and coastal positions shelled enemy gunsites. Under hazardous conditions, an orderly evacuation could be evidenced.

As the German advance closed in; the whole harbour was subjected to a 'baptism of fire'. Two destroyers at berth, *Keith* and *Vimy*, both lost their commanders. The commander of the Keith was killed on his bridge and the commander of the Vimy mortally wounded. Both destroyers left their berth, stern first and full of soldiers. Destroyers *Whitshed* and *Vimiera* went in and took off Irish and Welsh Guards and Royal Marines. With guns blazing about 1,000 left in each ship.

By now enemy tanks, guns and machine-guns were only a few hundred yards away. Yet again destroyers came to the rescue when *Wild Swan* and *Venemous* filled the berth. A third destroyer, *Venetia*, was ordered in. At the harbour entrance she received a hit and burst into flames.

German tanks seized the opportunity to open fire to finish her off. Should they succeed, *Venetia* would block the harbour entrance and *Wild Swan* and *Venemous* would be at their mercy. However, there was nothing wrong with *Venetia's guns as the enemy soon found out. Although on fire and making a heavy list, stern first she cleared the harbour, returning home to fight yet another day.*

The Germans now directed their fire-power on the destroyers at berth. Along the steep streets opposite the harbour, German tanks came clattering down. Now a swan is reputed to sing melodiously at the point of death. The German target was *Wild Swan* and her sister *Venemous*. The guns of *Wild Swan* erupted with the melody of success. Those of *Venemous* with much rancour. At point blank range, *Wild Swan* scored a direct hit on a leading tank. Surely, this must be an unparalled instance in any nation's naval history of a direct combat between a destroyer and a tank. Both destroyers, safely left harbour for England with about 1000 men apiece on board. Two years later, H.M.S. *Wild Swan* found herself facing heavy odds when attacked by twelve enemy planes. This time the enemy put an end to her. Those lethal guns fired until the very end, knocking four enemy planes out of the sky.

The end was in sight. Another destroyer, the *Windsor* arrived and took off a further 600 plus 30 wounded. The last ship to reach the besieged port was the *Vimiera*, on her second trip. She had entered during the dark hours and was on her way home shortly before daybreak. Over 1400 passengers embarked. In addition to soldiers, many were refugees. The fleeing Jews and Poles amongst the refugees were 'dead men' if they had been captured.

Almost the whole of the British force had got away. Under the command of Major Windsor Lewis, a small contingent held out for a further 24 hours. A staunch resistance had been manifested by the French at Ville Haute. The Germans demanded surrender otherwise they would level the town out. General Languetot had no alternative but to accede. He didn't know the British had departed and felt their action surreptitious.

On May 25th, Boulogne was in German hands.

CALAIS

The name of Calais was mentioned for the first time in a charter dated 1181, the town being a port of the County of Boulogne.

At the beginning of the 14th Century, the town was prosperous and an economic delight. England was a great trading neighbour.

Alas! War with England soon changed affairs. After the battle of Crecy, Edward III attacked Calais. Resistance was valiant and the English King soon realised how strongly fortified the town was. It took a whole year of blockade to force the starving town into surrender.

Edward's frustration grew into admiration and he showed mercy by sparing the people of Calais. However, there was a condition. Six of the richest Burghars must give themselves up to him. This was agreed and as specified they presented themselves, barefooted, dressed in long shirts, around each neck a hangman's noose. In their hands they held the Keys to the town. Execution faced them but due to the intervention of Queen Philippa de Hainaut, a pardon was granted.

For over 200 years, Calais remained an English possession. In 1558, to the complete surprise of the English occupation force, Calais was attacked and won back for France. The success was short lived, for in 1596 the Spanish forces launched an assault which succeeded. However, 2 years later it was given back to France under the terms of the Treaty of Vervins.

The lessons of history were noted by the people of Calais. Fully conscious of how near Spain and England were to them, the next hundred years saw major steps being taken to ensure the town had adequate defences.

During the first world war, the town defences were not tested through enemy invasion. Nevertheless, Calais became the recipient of many bombardments due to the constant troop movements to and from England.

Today, Calais is certified amongst the most important French passenger ports. Served by sea-routes from English ports, some 110 daily trips are made during the peak season. Of course, in recent years the advent of Hovercraft services from Dover and Ramsgate has greatly increased the cross-Channel traffic.

To stroll along the Boulevard Jacquard with its pleasant shops is a real pleasure. Here you will find the statue erected to the memory of Jacquard, to whom the town's lace industry is indebted. The Boulevard also leads to the Town Hall, worthy of a pause, if not only to admire Auguste Rodin's fine sculpture of the Six Burghars. Another worthwhile walk is down the rue du Duc de Guise, which brings you to the very old Notre Dame Church, where in 1921 Charles de Gaulle married Yvonne Vendroux.

Between May 22 and 26th 1940, sightseeing was far from the British Soldier's mind. To stop and admire the sculpture of the Six Burghars spelt instant death, as German soldiers sniped from the heights of the Town Hall building. Calais was no place for tourists.

While the battle for Boulogne was being enacted, a grim struggle for Calais took place. Facing overwhelming odds, the soldiers conducted themselves in a manner to match the finest traditions of the British Army. At Boulogne, 4,600 troops returned to England. The Calais story presents a different picture. The heroic defence of the town fell upon the shoulders of a battalion each of the Queen Victoria Rifles, together with a unit of Royal Artillery who manned the searchlight batteries. First to arrive from England were the Queen Victoria Rifles, a Territorial motor-cycle battalion. They arrived minus their motor-cycles and poorly armed, most of the men having been recruited from London's large drapery stores, the headquarters of the unit being in the West End. Their Commanding Officer Brigadier Nicholson had the task of commanding the entire defence force consisting of some three thousand British troops and about one thousand French troops.

Churchill was determined that the defence of Calais would be his shopwindow in an effort to demonstrate to France a continuation of the co-operation which hitherto had subsisted between the two nations. War Minister, Anthony Eden sent a radio message to Calais — "The eyes of the Empire are upon the defence of Calais." This summed up how Churchill felt. A few hours later Nicholson received a further message from Eden emphasising the value of every hour they continued to resist.

They were now engaging enemy forces en route for Dunkirk and the message underlined their continued activity as of the greatest help to the B.E.F. In later years, Churchill wrote concerning the decision not to order an evacuation but rather order them to fight on, that he felt, 'physically sick'. After all, to sacrifice so many lives is not an easy decision to make.

Churchill could see clearly what was happening as the soldiers of Calais bought valuable time at such a heavy price. General Guderian had three armoured divisions and two of these divisions were engaged at Calais. For the B.E.F., Dunkirk was now the only way home. The all important Gravelines waterline had to be held as part of the action in guarding the routes for the final withdrawal to Dunkirk. Brigadier Nicholson and his men helped to make it possible for the B.E.F. to reach Dunkirk.

The fighting soon was street by street. The Germans almost had to fight for every house. During the morning of Sunday, May 26th, the Germans under a flag of truce demanded the garrison's surrender. Should they fail to comply the alternative would be annihilation. The Brigadier was given a short time to deliberate. His reply, according to the Germans was 'The answer is NO!' Before the end of that day most of the town and the docks were destroyed. Everywhere buildings were ablaze; the town obscured by smoke.

Loss of life was high. Many soldiers wounded. Whilst Calais burned, the sniper unmercifully selected his prey and the bombardment of fire spat death and destruction everywhere, and ordinary men like Army Chaplain the Rev. Richard Craig found extraordinary abilities. Near Calais Docks Station he set up an aid-post. For three days he organised the dressing and evacuation of some 300 wounded. News was brought to him of six wounded men lying on the sand dunes. Due to enemy snipers they were pinned down. Without a second thought, the Chaplain asked for four volunteers and drove an ambulance to the locality. With his four helpers he crawled to the wounded men, transferred them to the ambulance and drove them back under fire. For his devotion to duty he was awarded the Military Cross.

By late afternoon on Sunday 26th May, the enemy had captured the whole of the docks area. In the old Citadel, British and French troops put up a strong resistance. Greatly outnumbered they fought on, suffering high casualties. Even the Germans commented, 'they fought with courage and desperation'.

With much haste, the Royal Navy worked industriously to evacuate the wounded. Although the destroyer *Wessex* was sunk by enemy bombers such efforts did not cease until the fighting ended and Calais capitulated. Only thirty unwounded men made their way back to England on Navy ships. Many of their comrades now lày dead in the streets of the town. Others were captured to spend the next five years of their life in a prison camp. The heroic commander Brigidier Claude Nicholson fought until he was completely surrounded. Sadly, he died in captivity with the belief that he had failed. If only he could have been informed of Mr. Churchill's speech made just nine days later. Addressing a crowded House of Commons, he said:—

27

... four days of intense street fighting passed before a silence reigned over Calais which marked the end of a memorable resistance. Their sacrifice was not, however, in vain. At last two armoured divisions, which otherwise would have been turned against the British Expeditionary Force, had to be sent there to overcome them. They added another page to the glories of the Light Division, and the time gained enabled the Gravelines waterline to be flooded and held by the French troops, and thus it was that the port of Dunkirk was kept open.

CHAPTER FOUR

Halt Befehl

The sudden order issued by Hitler which resulted in his armoured forces coming to a halt just outside Dunkirk has been the subject of much debate. At the time it was given — May 24th, the German Panzers had reached the Channel Coast behind the British Expeditionary Force and everything seemed to point at the likelihood of the British losing a vital race and finding themselves cut off from the sea. The intervention of Hitler held back the armoured forces, enabling the retreating British Army to escape. When taking into account the events of the previous two weeks culminating in the crushing of Holland and Belgium; the infliction of severe losses upon French and British forces, it appears quite out of character for the story to have such an ending. If Hitler had followed his lightning pattern of conquest and allowed the dreaded Panzers to continue, General Guderian would have broken through the shrinking Allied perimeter and reached Dunkirk on the evening of the 25th.

Many thinking and learned people have asked the simple question: 'why did Hitler stop?' All historians record the fact and yet those who have felt challenged to interpret Hitler's action are of multivarious opinion. The whole affair bears the mark of incredibility that a 'halt order' should go forth at a time when British and French forces were battle worn and weary; the British Expeditionary Force confronted with the frightening situation of encirclement having already experienced a severence of communication with its bases and German armour poised to block the way in its retreat to the sea.

A study of the salient features of interpretation reveal interesting conclusions, yet at the same time serve to underline the widespread diversity of view. The analytical data appertaining to the main line arguments could be summed up as follows:—

Firstly, a school of thought promulgates the idea of Hitler wishing to spare the British Expeditionary Force the humiliation of defeat and surrender. Putting a stop to the tanks would soften the situation; the underlying motive a preparatory step in bringing to fruition an honourable settlement with the British.

Whilst some dismiss such an opinion without a second glance, there are aspects which cannot so easily be overlooked. It is lucidly clear in Hitler's *Mein Kampf*, he held the British in high esteem, not classifying them amongst future enemies. Sixteen years had elapsed since the book's publication but this did not mean the convictions of the author were changed. After all, he felt the same about the Italians, who at that time were not involved in the war but considered an ally.

Like a whirlwind the might of Germany caused a wave of devestation which overwhelmed Poland in 17 days; Denmark, 2 days; Norway, 24 days; Holland, 5 days and Belgium in 17 days. Why then should Hitler suddenly pause in the midst of a successful campaign? Especially when he enjoyed much admiration from new converts drawn from the ranks of his military advisors. Profusely, they had disagreed with the strategy of their Fuhrer but the manner in which a large slice of Europe was struck down caused respect to be directed where due. Their applause was his meat and drink. One thing is quite certain — Hitler had not gone soft. Quite the contrary, he not only thought himself right but intended to demonstrate it to the world. History would declare him not only a great military conqueror but equally a political genius. Hitler considered Britain more than a small island of nuisance value; she was the head of a huge Empire, the base of an admirable civilisation, the preservation of which was sorely needed. To be at peace with the British Empire, having gained her recognition of Germany's position in Europe, would surely exhibit political expertise. Obviously, the annihilation of the British Expeditionary Force would more than infuriate the whole of the British Empire. With certainty, a people steeped in a heritage of 'honour' must regard the destruction of her army as far from being conducive to good future relations.

A second view points out the plain commonsense of halting the tanks at the Canal line. The geography beyond this point presented conditions unfavourable to heavy armour. During the First World War, Hitler as a serving soldier took note of the difficulties tanks experienced in swamp-like conditions. Now the fear of his depleted tank force finding itself bogged down in the tract of country around Dunkirk, presented a realistic eventuality. This anxiety can be understood, for at that time the tank force was down to 50% of strength attributable to losses sustained in combat and an increasing number of breakdowns.

The moment had arrived for the mechanics to take over; to build up the armoured strength for the second phase of the Battle of France. Hitler's eye was fixed upon the French capital, Paris, and not Dunkirk. The Battle of Flanders was as good as won — now for the Battle of France.

Through Hitler's eyes, the British Army, once a formidable opponent but now in full retreat, would not come back into the war. He would kill and capture as many British servicemen as possible; those who escaped need not make much of their freedom, for everyone in the British Isles had their days numbered. After having driven the British Navy from the English Channel, sweeping the channel clear of mines, a blockade was envisaged to the limit of imprisoning Britons in their own island home.

The third oft supported argument focuses the spotlight on Hermann Goring the uncrowned King of the 'egotists'. Goring, a survivor of many aerial combats in World War One, receiving acclaim as an air-ace, was the head of the German Luftwaffe and a personal friend of Hitler. Now he wanted to persuade his Fuhrer that the achievement of the mechanized land *blitzkrieg* could receive its 'crown of glory' as his Messerschmitt's, Junkers, Stukas finished off the fleeing armies, not only striking terror and destruction but making any sea rescue attempt a nigh impossibility.

This was no wild scheme, for even Churchill publicly stated in his estimation no more than 20-30,000 had any chance of getting away from the beaches due to the extreme vulnerability of the open sands and rescue ships to air attack.

The historians in their search for an answer to this extremely puzzling situation, intensify the mystery with their discussion of the source of the order upon which German tanks came to a halt. Who really issued the command to stand still outside Dunkirk with instructions not to pass the Lens — Bethune — St. Omer — Gravelines line?

Some express doubt as to whether this oft debated order emanated from Hitler at all. Winston Churchill is categorical in stating the resultant action was due to the initiative of Field-Marshall von Runstedt. On the morning of May 24th, Hitler paid a visit to Charleville, the Headquarters of von Runstedt and consequent upon their meeting an immediate order went out prohibiting the passing of the Canal line.

It is true von Rundstedt feared the French Commander intended to take the advantage through launching attacks upon his widely dispersed forces and Hitler shared this uneasiness. Also, von Rudstedt made no secret of wanting a peace settlement with Britain. Upon this issue, historians differ considerably. To gather their opinions and publish them in one volume they would make a chronicle of utter confusion. A popular question goes to the heart of the situation: 'If von Rundstedt had prompted Hitler to proclaim the "halt order", why then did Hitler not later place the blame upon him for the British escape?' Indeed ! An apt and straight to the point question, for to cast the blame elsewhere characterises Hitler's personality.

I think the explanation is simple when accepting the evidence from both von Rudstedt and Hitler sharing common fears and desires. Both feared continuing the armoured thrust for reasons already discussed and especially in the light of their suspicions regarding a possible manoeuvre by the French Commander; both desired an early settlement with the British. When two people are in agreement there is nothing at all to argue about. I believe on this occasion both men spoke the same language and it was normal and inevitable for Hitler as Commander-in-Chief, having received the confirmation he sought, then to treat the decision as his own.

Sincere writers in their search for a cause to Hitler's hesitation are at least in agreement with the outcome — it saved the British Army. Unfortunately, none have taken into account the complex character of Hitler in an effort to ascertain the reason for his decision. Or furnished space to the call by King George VI on May 24th, (the day the tanks came to a halt) for the nation to hold a National Day of Prayer. The neglect of these two important affairs necessitates such variation of opinion and ambiguity of thought in the pursuit to find a logical answer. Even today, the application of terminology like, 'the miracle of Dunkirk', and 'the Dunkirk Spirit' falls from the lips of people acutely conscious of the narrowness of the escape, yet still ignorant of its cause.

It is not by accident the word, 'miracle', which means, 'an act of supernatural power', has found permanent status in the Dunkirk story. In fact, the narrative is incomplete by any such exclusion and even after all these years recognition of what actually happened is still not fully appreciated.

As a young man, Hitler became fascinated by occultism — finding his interests in astrology and hypnotism. Occultism is defined as 'beyond the bounds of ordinary knowledge, mysterious, concealed, or hidden from view; belonging to certain reputed sciences, such as magic, astrology and various other practices. Astrology became Hitler's darling passion — his faith and resulted in a serious programming of his life. Now astrology is a study of the stars in order to determine their effect upon human affairs. The position of the stars at birth, is said to be the factor in determining the course of a person's life. This method of fortune-telling appealed to Hitler delighting in horoscope readings for security and advice.

In discussing astrology, care must be exercised in separating it from astronomy, a legitimate field of study. Astrology began about 5,000 years ago when people worshipped the sun, moon, and the five known planets of that time as gods. They thought between them they owned the heavens, each dwelling in his own house. Later the notion developed and the zodiac established, this being an imaginary belt of the heavens outside of which the sun, moon and major planets do not pass. Divided crosswise into twelve equal areas called signs of the zodiac, these became twelve 'houses'. Because the sun and moon represented night and day they were allocated one 'house' each. The remaining ten 'houses' were assigned to the five planets, namely Venus, Saturn, Mars, Jupiter and Mercury. One for the day and another for the night.

The so-called "astrological science" flourished until the late eighteenth century. Then for over a hundred years it remained little practiced until its revival in France and Britain at the close of the nineteenth century and in Germany about 1925. Hitler, fascinated by the subject, soon became obsessed with it, relying on the illogical and irrational. Astrology was now a religion to him; with conviction he believed the prognostications and advice of astrologers. The astrologer's 'chart' or 'horoscope' for May 10th, 1940, the day on which he launched his attack upon Belgium, Holland and Luxemburg, revealed a successful conclusion to any project undertaken.

Hitler showed his faith and struck. Intoxicated by the plaudits of his friends, *Grosster Feldherr aller Zeiten* — the greatest general of all time, he felt himself to be a prophet, strangely fulfilling the flashes of prophetic revelations he believed had been imparted. Whereas the Christian has the Bible, Hitler looked upon *Mein Kampf* as a repository of truth, a book of prophecy incontestably avouched. Much of the Apostle Paul's inspiration and writings at inception proceeded from a prison cell, likewise, *Mein Kampf*, penned from a prison cell, in the author's mind was nothing less than a library filled with ethnology, ethics, prophecy, political science and absolute rules for personal and social life.

The 'halt order' at the decisive hour before Dunkirk although strikingly opportune from an Allied point of view, nevertheless just had to happen. Hitler set himself up for it! He firmly believed that he was the greatest general history could produce; following the success of the thrust through the Ardennes, generals who then privately thought him completely mad were now shouting his praises. Hitler loved it! Like an actor strutting upon the world's stage, Hitler now intended all to witness a master political genius at work, for rooted in his mind were the declarations made in *Mein Kampf* concerning the English. In a short space of time prophecies made some sixteen years previously were finding fulfilment. As promised, the 'Jewish problem', which he described as a 'threat' to racial purity and strength, was now being dealt with. Hitler declared that ancient civilizations crumbled because the 'racial blood' was adulterated. Superior weapons did not necessarily indicate a superior nation but rather a nation's greatness depended on the quality of its powers of resistance.

Now as Fuehrer, he determined, let providence write the sequel to *Mein Kampf* upon the pages of history. Something like the Old Testament and the New Testament with Hitler playing the roll of Messiah.

The Bible is a complete book, the Old Testament unfolded in

the New and the New Testament enfolded in the Old. Hitler intended all his prophecies to come true and unfold themselves by the creation of a new Germany. Indubitably, time in no way dimmed the vision; the vow to destroy the French he was keeping, the incorporation of all European Germans into the Greater Reich with brilliance he achieved by annexing Austria, Danzig, Czecholovakia and the Saar.

Perhaps the meeting with von Rudstedt and subsequent 'halt order', is better understood against the background *Mein Kampf* provides. A re-enaction of the meeting spotlights a deeply superstitious Hitler, someone who believed in good and bad omens. To hear von Rundstedt expressing anxiety over a possible French attack hit him like a rocket. At this stage nothing could go wrong, he must keep his promise and conquer France — his eye and heart were set upon Paris. Through his mind would echo the voices of those around him, recapturing their opinions and causing confusion in his already passive mind. In von Rundstedt, Hitler found a 'good omen'. Here was a man who desired peace with the English, confirmed his fears regarding a subtle French manoeuvre and generally spoke the sense he wished to hear. So he stopped the tanks as his eye was on Paris — not Dunkirk. Obviously he knew the retreating British would have a somewhat sporting chance of making it home which in his mind took the shape of a better proposition than complete annihilation. To dent British pride totally in no way appeared proper behaviour for a German Empire of the future to raise her eagle's head, glance across the English Channel and receive an acknowledgement of friendship from the English.

The horoscope of May 10th, launched Hitler on wings of promise, it also moulded his personality. Apart from other considerations, which will be considered later, a psychological result amongst people with a predisposition to believe the horoscope is the power of suggestion made to the mind. Predictions often come true because they are accepted with a childlike faith. Here is guidance, meaning and security on demand. Like a tender plant it becomes rooted, in the mind, compelling the seeker by suggestion to order his life according to the horoscope, thus the prediction often comes true because you allow it to do so.

Subjection to horoscopes is an addiction with allied consequences as untoward as addiction to alcohol or drugs. It binds the human will effectively as a chain placed around due to the degree of auto suggestion which sows ideas into the subconscious mind. It stupifies ability to make decisions, destroys initiative and hampers judgement. Such was Hitler's condition on May 24th. German War Diaries recorded around that time cast a glimpse of Hitler manifesting nervous behaviour — frightened by his own success — afraid to take chances — raging and screaming at any with ideas contrary to his own, warning them they have thoughts capable of ruining the whole campaign. Is it any wonder diarists took note of his behaviour? I'm sure 'exitement' mingled in the mysterious and complex personality of Adolf Hitler. The horoscope promised a successful conclusion and he believed it! Even remarks like, 'the war will be over in six weeks', conclusively illustrate the sanguine disposition of this astrological slave.

The 24th May, 1940 fell on a Friday, which to superstitious people is not for decision making, anyhow. But King George VI having amongst his titles, 'Defender of the Faith' felt otherwise. This was 'Empire Day' and he would turn it into 'Decision Day' when the whole Empire shared the burden of the King's heart. Upon the King's heart lay the answer — call the people to a National Day of Prayer. Solemnly, he decreed, Sunday, May 26th, would be set aside for this sacred purpose. The Hand of God was against Adolf Hitler.

At 9 p.m. the B.B.C. Home and Overseas Service delivered the King's Message to the Empire.

> ... The decisive struggle is now upon us. I am going to speak plainly to you, for in this hour of trial I know that you would not have me do otherwise.
>
> Let no one be mistaken: it is no mere territorial conquest that our enemies are seeking. It is the overthrow, complete and final, of this Empire and everything for which it stands; and after that the conquest of the world. And if their will prevails they will bring to its accomplishment all the hatred and cruelty which they have already displayed. It was not easy for us to believe that designs so evil could find a place in the human mind but the time for doubt is long past.
>
> ... To all of us this Empire, to all men of vision and good will throughout the world the issue is now plain: it is life or death for us all... I speak to you today with a new vision of this Empire before my eyes. Now that it has come into conflict and sharp comparison with the evil system which is attempting its destruction, its full significance appears in a brighter and more certain light. ...
>
> Against our honesty is set dishonour, against our faithfulness is set treachery, against our justice brute force...
>
> At this fateful hour we turn, as our fathers before us have turned in all times of trial, to God Most High. Here in the old country I have asked that Sunday next should be observed as a Day of National Prayer. It may be possible for many of our brothers across the seas to join their prayers with ours.
>
> Let us with one heart and soul humbly but confidently commit our cause to God and ask His aid that we may valiantly defend the right as it is given to us to see it. ...
>
> Keep your hearts proud and your resolve unshaken. Let us go

forward to that task as one man a smile on our lips and our heads held high, and with God's help we shall not fail.

CHAPTER FIVE

The National Day of Prayer

The announcement that His Majesty the King had expressed a desire for a National Day of Prayer resulted in rejoicing amongst many who with fervour acclaimed the initiative taken. Shouldn't the Christians have been praying anyway? Is an oft repeated question but the very fact of Christians at prayer brought about the National Day of Prayer. Throughout the nation Christian leaders voiced a conviction similar to the message King Solomon received from God:

> If my people which are called by My name shall humble themselves and pray and seek My face and turn from their wicked ways, then will I hear from heaven and will forgive their sin and will heal their land.

In a statement issued on the 17th April, 1940, the Archbishop of Canterbury, the Moderator of the General Assembly of the Church of Scotland, and the Moderator of the Federal Council of Evangelical Free Churches, asked that Prayer should be said "that the rule of force may be overcome and that truth, mercy, freedom and justice may be established amongst nations."

Everywhere, Christians came against the tide of evil in the might and power of prayer. In addition to the prayers offered up on a Sunday when the people assembled at God's House, midweek prayer groups mushroomed. Half-night and whole-night prayer meetings took place, many convened in private homes, as God's people interceded on behalf of the nation. But this was not enough for some! A constant stream of letters addressed to the King, others to the Prime Minister exhorted — A National Day of Prayer. Newspapers carried advertisements: "Why Not a Day of National Prayer?" Another: "Wake-up, Britain, and acknowledge publicly your real leader, who will bring us victory."

Conviction grew. Pressure mounted at the same time as arguments raged. Not all Christians shared the vision of a National Day of Prayer disputing the validity of inviting the ungodly to make a convenience of the church and pray to a God who rarely enters their thoughts. Each Sunday throughout the Empire prayers about the situation were being offered up, so voices here and there resounded to the effect that this was adequate. After all, the Christians were doing the praying, what more could be asked? Naturally, belligerants enjoyed a field day with the question: "If the Nazis seek Divine help — what then?" Nevertheless, men of vision from all walks of life felt strongly guided in spending their energies to this end. In the House of Commons, Sir Ernest Little asked the Prime Minister whether "a day of prayer would be set apart when the whole nation would be called to prayer for Divine help to enable us to overthrow the enemy, and to promote such a spirit of brotherhood and good will among the nations of the earth, that they will seek war no more."

Few understand the character of a National Day of Prayer, explaining the event as a publicity drive by the churches. Actually, the position is quite the contrary. The calling of a 'solemn assembly' heralds a gesture indicative of a national approach to God in an official Act of State. The full import not realised unless appreciative acceptation of the fact is granted of the King carrying out this role as Head of Church and State. It must be a day called by desire of the King, for he alone properly represents the nation. The King accompanied by the Ministers of the Crown and members of both Houses of Parliament, the official representatives of the people, together with the leaders of the Christian Churches formulates a national approach to God. Through their mediatorial action the whole nation is represented officially. Just as the sun shines upon the godly as well as the ungodly, all reap the benefits whether they joined in the intercession or not.

Prayer is force and prayer changes things because it links man's petition to the power of God. There is passion in the praying that prevails and the people of Britain like Israel of old turned to the God of Abraham. Newspaper articles like the Daily Mirror's, 'Face the Facts' warned: "We are in greater peril than we were at any moment in the last great war". In a speech, Mr. Churchill prepared the nation to bear the burden of "hard and heavy tidings." A member of Parliament asked, "Is this Armageddon?"

On Sunday, 26th May, the King attended Westminster Abbey for the solemn hour of intercession. Perhaps as he looked around recognising members of the Cabinet, the House of Commons, House of Lords and the leaders of the Churches he would feel awed by the occasion. Especially at the thought of his subjects throughout the Nation and Empire making their way to the House of God to join their King in prayer. No doubt he would recall how as a young man he watched his father, the late King George V lead a similar procession at St. Margarets, Westminster. The date being 4th August, 1918, the fourth anniversary of Britain's hostilities with Germany and a day when the King led the Nation to Prayer.

The morale of the British people was at a low ebb due to the stri-

Thou hast given a great Deliverance

king gains the Germans had accomplished. Some six months previously Ludendorff launched a massive offensive — the *Kaiserschlacht* (Emperor battle). British losses were alarming as the German's broke through part of the line held by the Fifth Army. Ludendorff's master stroke caused consternation in the Allied camp. Germany seemed to be winning the war.

On 17th July, the British Prime Minister announced in the House of Commons that 4th August would be a National Day of Prayer. The very next day the new Allied Supreme Commander, Marshall Foch initiated the Allied counter-offensive with an attack led by tanks at Villers — Cotterets.

The French commenced an advance which would not let up until the Armistice was signed. German Count Hertling stated: "On the 18th day of July, 1918, the most optimistic of us became convinced that all was lost. The history of the world was altered in three days."

On 8th August, four days after the National Day of Prayer, British Commander-in-Chief, Sir Douglas Haig launched an attack which completely surprised the Germans. Shortly after 4 a.m. under cover of a thick mist, 500 tanks commenced the offensive. At the end of that first day the British Army progressed more than in any previous first-day engagement. The Germans were astounded counting in one day 27,000 men killed, wounded and missing. They searched for a reason to account for the remarkable change of fortune. "The Allies were favoured by a thick fog", said one report. However, a more thoughtful Lunderdorff called it, "the blackest day of the German army in the history of the war". In a miraculous way the tide of war changed. During September, Lunderdorff told the Kaiser that Germany was defeated. Finally, on November 11th, 1918, an Armistice was signed. The greatest war Britain had yet fought was over.

What had happened? On August 4th, defeat stared the nation in the face, yet three months later she was at peace. The nation as a whole seemed to have been enlivened and brought under the influence of a new spirit. It affected the British Commander-in-Chief, Sir Douglas Haig when he launched the second Battle of the Somme. Two years previously he had been Commander-in-Chief at the first Battle of the Somme, yet what an amazing contrast.

A vital consequence of a National Day of Prayer is not so much what God may do because of the intercession but the spiritual transformation which is induced in the nation. Prayer certainly changes things with far reaching effects. Not so far, however, as changing the character of God. For example, God is always ready to forgive a repentent sinner. Now repentence is the conditioning factor which represents a different feeling or attitude in the life of the one seeking forgiveness. It is fallacy of thought to believe the prayer of a repentent alters the mind of God. Because the mind of

God is always set upon pardoning the sinner subject to fulfilment of the condition, i.e. repentence. Therefore, the change entirely takes place on the human level when prayer leads to conviction and generates purpose which in turn signposts energy the seedbed of activity. And by faith the repentent sinner accepts God's pardon. The first miracle of prayer is scenic in the human personality and precedes a miracle in nature. As in the case of the repentent, prayer has creative powers producing a situation whereby it is right or proper for God to issue his pardon.

Likewise, the first result of a national approach to God is the miracle in the personality of the nation as a whole; the nation becoming a channel through which God's power can flow. Such was the desire of King George VI, a godly man, inspiring and leading millions of subjects throughout the Nation and Empire to the Throne of the King of Kings. On the evening of the day Britain entered the war, he told the nation: ". . . with God's help, we shall prevail". Whilst the King and people prayed, the German High Command boasted: "The British Army is encircled." A dark hour was upon Britain, the blackness of the position revealed in a speech by the Prime Minister, nine days later on June 4th, the last day of the evacuation:

> When a week ago today I asked the House to fix this afternoon as the occasion for a statement, I feared it would be my hard lot to announce the greatest military disaster in our long history. I thought — and some good judges agreed with me — that perhaps 20,000 or 30,000 men might be re-embarked. . . . The whole root and core and brain of the British Army, on which and around which we were to build the Great British Armies in the later years of the war, seemed about to perish upon the field, or to be led into ignominious and starving captivity. That was the prospect a week ago.

But a miracle happened. Churchill called it: "a miracle of deliverance." From a seeming hopeless position over 335,000 men were brought home. In the sky the Royal Air Force inflicted upon the enemy losses of at least four to one as the navy using almost 1,000 ships of varying descriptions ferried the men home. Even yachts and barges joined the strange convoy as nature itself extended a helping hand. Rarely has the English Channel offered such calm waters for so long a period of time. God was at work in answer to prayer, "when he gave to the sea his decree." Or as the hymn writer puts it: "The winds and the waves shall obey His Will, Peace be Still."

The weather again aided the troops on the 28th as a violent storm broke out over Flanders providing cover for the men in their withdrawal to Dunkirk. The German News Agency in its daily commentary on the war stated: "Conditions unfavourable for the employment of great numbers of aircraft are assisting the fugitives." But Sunday newspaper, 'The Dispatch' of June 2nd said:

> Hammered on three sides and in danger of losing the coastal ports which remained their only chance of withdrawal, they attempted the greatest military feat in history.
> Could they escape overwhelming disaster? It seemed unlikely.
> But then two things happened:—

> First, the English Channel, that notorious rough stretch of water, became as calm and smooth as a pond. In consequence, not only large steamers but all kinds of small craft, including even river barges were able to cross to Dunkirk, carrying thousands of troops to safety. Secondly, while the smooth sea was aiding our ships, a fog was concealing our troops from the devastating attacks by the enemy's air strength.

The Dispatch concluded the article by saying: "Perhaps you who read this will go to your Church today."

Many did. Britain seemed to come alive! A newspaper claimed that: "The King's call to prayer and the tribulations of the past week have brought a spiritual reawakening to Britain." They did not hold 'conferences on prayer', or 'teach-ins'. They prayed and continued to pray. The Bible says, 'let us come before His face with thanksgiving' and 'with thanksgiving let your requests be made known unto God.' Sunday, 9th June dawned and evidenced King and people going up to the House of God with thanksgiving upon their hearts and expression of their lips.

There can be no doubt that God answers prayer. The promises of the Bible are explicit to those who pray. A Dunkirk history minus the King and people at prayer will not suffice. Who can appreciate the 'miracle of deliverance' by the exclusion of this important day? The historians dilemma of the previous chapter is one fruit of its unfortunate omission. Some will contend the German 'halt order' resounded two full days before the National Day of Prayer, debating any relevance whatsoever. The day the King announced his intention for the 26th May, the German armour came to a stop. The Bible says 'And it shall come to pass, that before they call, I will answer; and while they are yet speaking, I will hear!" Two wonderful promises, firstly, in anticipation of the call to be made, and answer is supplied witnessed in the 'halt order'. Secondly, the latter part of the verse describes a people speaking to God who hears their cry. It is significant to note, 'Operation Dynamo' resulting in 335,000 men coming home, was launched on the same day Britain prayed.

Something else happened which changed the face of history. Hitler up to the 24th May, in spite of his megalomania seasoned with bouts of melancholia, proved his capability in arriving at clear headed decisions, oftentimes brilliant military ventures. For years his cunning scheming mind more than matched statesmen of the highest quality. His hypnotic personality issuing an arrestive magnetism. Hitler possessed an unusual power for executing major decisions on the basis of intuition, time and again proving to doubters around him the correctness of his action. Only the previous Christmas, journalist Count von Schewerin wrote: 'The Fuehrer is to the German people what Christ was to the world of nearly 2,000 years ago — the messenger of the Almighty. . . .' At Dunkirk, the German Messiah lost his way. The war he thought almost won turned into a lost cause: it was the beginning of the path to destruction rather than salvation. The name 'Dunkirk' should be written in letters of gold with the date of 24th May declared a red letter day in the history of World War II and indeed in the history of mankind.

Someone once wrote a book entitled, 'Man's Extremity is God's Opportunity!' And the New Testament announces: "we know not what we should pray for as we ought." In times of need our prayers include petitions in the area of what is urgent and obvious. But often what stares us in the face does not present the complete picture simply because we do not see far enough.

Britain stood in need of deliverance, yet the people, through no fault of their own were not aware of whom they were really dealing with and ignorant of the real need. The Apostle Paul sheds light upon the heart of the matter when he states: "we wrestle not against flesh and blood, but against principalities, against powers, against the rulers of the darkness of this world, against spiritual wickedness in high places." Which leads to an obvious question:— was Hitler demon-possessed? An instrument through which the powers of darkness engaged themselves in seeking to unload their vengeance upon humanity? It is true, Hitler detested Christianity, "One is either a German or a Christian. You cannot be both." Early in the war a Church of England Bishop remarked: "There are no Christians among many of the German airmen captured in this country." Prisoners were asked to state their religion and 50 per cent answered 'Nature', 40 per cent replied 'Hitler' and 10 per cent said they were atheists. 'Nature' indicated a worship of ancient Teuton gods.

In 1834, Heine the great German Jewish poet, whose books Hitler banned, wrote:

> Christianity has occasionally calmed the brutal German lust for battle, but cannot destroy that savage joy. And when once that restraining talisman, the Cross, is broken, the old stone gods will rise from unremembered ruins and Thor will leap to life again and bring down his gigantic hammer upon the Gothic cathedrals.

The emblem of the god Thor was a hammer of gold, designated

prior to the present century as the 'Fylfot cross'. Today, we recognise it as 'a swastika'. Legend portrays the 'Hammer of Thor' a deadly projectile when thrown. Accurately, it found its target and always returned to the thrower's hand.

Early in the twentieth century, the swastika underwent a revival of attraction to the German. Commercially, a good proposition as a number of firms manufactured swastika badges and belt-buckles, Hitler viewed it with delight in his search for a design to symbolise himself and his cause. Finally, he settled for a swastika on a white disc against a red background. Dr. Friedrick Krohn came up with the appealing design. However, Krohn, an occultist, didn't have the last say in the matter. Hitler did. Hitherto, the Swastika assumed a right-handed form. Hitler wanted something entirely new so he changed it to the now familiar left-handed sawstika.

Under the banner of the swastika, the German brought to light the legend of Thor. With evil intent throwing its 'hammer-force' against the countries of Europe and striking down with incredible accuracy every object at which it aimed. When it came to Britain's turn the hammer did not return to the hand of the thrower as in previous instances. This time it flew back to strike Hitler down. The Old Testament prophet Jeremiah in describing the overthrow of the Babylon system employs choice and applicable words, "How is the hammer of the whole earth cut asunder and broken. . . . The Lord hath opened his armoury, and hath brought forth the weapons of his indignation." Hitler wielded it but it returned as the Hammer of God's Indignation.

The Nazi Party was riddled with leading associates of Hitler who had become fascinated with the occult. Not only intrigued but subjected. The Bible tells us that occultism is an abomination to the Lord because it is a forbidden realm and anyone who enters into Satan's domain by committing sins of sorcery not only abandons God but signs a contract with the Devil. S.S. leader Heinrich Himmler in the 1920's abandoned the Roman Catholic Church in order to dabble in sorcery. In the late 1930's rumour spread of his ambition to occupy the Seat of Grand Master of German occultism. He was weird and a strong believer in reincarnation actually perpetrating himself as the reincarnation of a Saxon monarch. Rudolf Hess, the deputy leader of the Nazi Party constantly consulted astrologers, clairvoyants and in particular those who dealt in cartomancy (fortune-telling, through the use of cards). Of complex nature, given to strange behaviour, constantly drinking in what the 'stars' had to say, disorder and despair assumed control of his life. On May 10th, 1941, he confounded them all by stealing a plane and flying to Scotland. Running out of fuel, he baled out and surrendered. When questioned, he revealed his identity claiming a special mission to the Duke of Hamilton. As the Duke listened, with authority Hess explained his mission. The whole idea of the flight originated with Hitler who wished to lay before the British people terms for peace. Concisely, he outlined the terms. In Germany the reaction was one of astonishment. Many, including the Fuehrer thought Hess to have undergone a brain disorder or been hypnotised by an occultist of other persuasion. And acting in a confused manner, compulsive thought led to the mission.

The German and British press gave credence to the line of thought that Hess's action found its source in astrology. Here on Scottish soil paraded another slave and victim of this unhealthy pre-occupation. The date chosen for the unfruitful journey is very interesting — May 10th. Twelve months previously to the actual date, Hitler launched his offensive through the Ardennes upon Holland and Belgium. As already discussed Hitler's horoscope revealed a "successful conclusion". Hess felt differently due to the influence of a number of prognasticators. Now unable to help himself they set him up to believe Hitler's future pronounced dark forebodings, whilst his own glimmered with the bright lights of success as he went forth to be an instrument of peace. Somewhere in his mixed up mind actual truth held sway in that Germany's future did not appear prosperous. It was if he wished to put back the clock one year and make May 10th eventuate a 'successful conclusion'.

The faith of a Christian is based upon solid facts — the life, death and resurrection of Jesus Christ. When a person becomes a Christian his character is changed, an assurance of salvation is given, the fruits of God's spirit take root in his life. Daily he looks for the protecting Hand of God upon him: the Christian knows the meaning of peace — with God, himself and as far as possible with his neighbour. In contrast, occultly subjected people not only abandon God but themselves. Exposing their lives to other influences. Hess illustrates the disintegration of the whole man activated by these unlawful persuits. Never at peace with himself, given to unusual behaviour and the development of psychic disturbances. As Christianity affects character, producing the blessed fruits of God, likewise subjection to the 'powers of darkness' affects the character of the person concerned. Exhibitions of bad temper, quarrelsomeness, confusion, compulsive habits, dominance, hallucination, voices, depressions, compile just a few items by which adherents are plagued.

The people of Britain would not trust a Prime Minister sometimes seen weeping like a child if he doesn't get his own way. One week calm and charming, the next hysterical and ranting. Speaking of hearing 'voices' unexplainable or appearing on television to talk about his latest premonition together with the recent thoughts about ending it all by committing suicide. Any Opposition Party would first of all pinch itself in an endeavour to ascertain if this could be reality or a dream. Certainly, the House of

Commons would echo the cry of 'Resign!' Who could trust such a man to exercise commonsense judgements? Furthermore, the strain of office would be too much; he would crack. Especially in the hour of crisis the nation would shudder and never envisage this type of leader capable of sound decision.

The aforementioned, truly describes Adolf Hitler. Yet in spite of it all he demonstrated an uncanny trait of cool decision enforced by conviction with startling result. Continually surrounded and controlled by dark powers, practised in black magic, the devil found a disciple worthy of executing foul deeds upon humanity. Abaddon means destruction, Apollyon the exterminator, Biblical names for Satan. The Scriptures show him to be subtle, deceitful, fierce, proud, powerful and wicked. Characteristics Hitler developed in his progress toward graduation from the devils school. He was the 'Hammer of Thor'.

During the years of my pastoral ministry I have counselled people in just about every circumstance of life. Not all have approached me with pure intentions. Like the man telephoning during the early hours of the morning simply to advise me I was wrestling with major problems. Naturally the man would receive full marks for accuracy. As he would if he persisted in putting the blunt statement to other Ministers of the Gospel, for the work of a true pastor is people and where one finds people one finds problems.

Believing the caller eventually would get to the point, I exercised my normal procedure in speaking little. Experience having taught a good listener is an essential requirement to effective pastoral counselling. Sensing the one on the other end of the line either under the influence of drugs or alcohol, due to the long pauses in conversation and slurred speech, I suggested he rang at a more reasonable time or even met me face to face. All next day I felt unusually tired and bemoaned the miserable spirit borne. Something quite foreign to me. I put it down to a disturbed night's rest. A couple of days later again I had to get up in the early hours of the morning to answer the telephone. Immediately I recognised the same voice minus the slur. He continued the theme of my having problems describing in fairly reasonable detail a matter of absolute confidence. Making no comment I asked him about his own problem as it became apparent through his choice of words this was no crank but an educated being, in a lot of trouble with himself. For some five minutes, punctuated with long pauses, he ranted on as if speech making on a platform about metaphysical phenomenon and other branches of parapsychology. Beneath the veneer I detected someone hopelessly at odds with himself. He agreed to meet me the next night but not in a church building, so we chose a venue in the town centre. On time I arrived at the late night cafe, waited an hour then returned home. I was not surprised when he didn't keep the appointment as all that day it seemed as if I knew he would not show up at the rendezvous. In fact I was glad to return home as once more following his early morning call I felt drained of energy, dis-spirited; the feeling enjoined when you lose a dear possession.

Suddenly, I knew the reason of the tiredness, loss of vitality and low spirits. I was a victim. Deliberately, the caller caused long pauses in our telephone talks. Not that he was lost for words or engaged in thought. By devious design he utilised the time in engaging himself as a type of telepathic 'Raffles'. It was a break-in. Without permission, from my mind he received thoughts and knowledge which I did not wish to impart. Getting me out of bed would not find me too alert especially choosing hours when medically speaking the body is at its lowest resistance. The energies he lacked through misuse of his own body in ungodly living he attempted to replenish by drawing upon mine. I decided upon a plan of action. Sure as clockwork, the familiar early morning ring sounded. Expecting his call, with the excuse of tendering sincere apologies for not keeping our appointment, I didn't go to bed, but waited. He went through the expected formalities, silently I prayed and came against the evil in the name of Jesus Christ. He began to shout and scream: "I can't get through!" I could hear him violently thumping with his hand the telephone kiosk coin box, repeatedly screaming: "I can't think!"

The man telephoned on subsequent occasions and piece by piece I formulated a sad human story. Through occult experimentation and the application of his learned mind to books on magic, this poor soul thought he was climbing the ladder of progress whilst all the time he was descending to a hell of his own conniving. Constantly hearing voices, footsteps behind him, he lacked peace in his life. Many days he underwent a state of grave anxiety with depression. Thoughts of suicide ran amok as he took to alcohol as a way out to quieten his blasphemous thoughts. Fear and disorder loaded his life.

I mention this one case history to bring to light an understanding of Hitler's behaviour when regulated by the force of a Nation's prayers.

Counterpart to the character in question he demonstrated psychic powers, particularly gifted in hypnotic sway. In addressing the masses he didn't really brain-wash them, he drew the very worst out of man. Others, who out of necessity conferred with the Fuehrer, testify to a combat of mind and will. On occasions the suggestive powers of Hitler rendered inert personal initiative, producing blind obedience and manifesting a faith within the zombi-typed adherents in believing Germany's new deliverer piloted them to a utopian age.

Unknown to Hitler the road he trod led to destruction, chaos and darkness. Already his occult dabblings took their toll by creating a 'monster', a title invested upon him by the British press. Whereas Christianity enables followers to proclaim: "Not my will but Thine be done!" Yet at the same time leaving the follower in full control of the power of decision due to the freedom brought by Christ. -Devilry also demands allegience but the human will is taken over and the follower subjected to slavery. Hitler, viewed in his dynamic magnetism, uncompromising drive, nevertheless was a slave to the Master he had chosen. Hate filled his life together with fear and its ensuing hang-ups.

The Bible says: "Fear hath torment". Which reminds me of a young Irishman who called upon me for counselling. Following a visit to a fortune-teller he was warned of three imminent happenings in his life. Quite soon, he was informed, a journey would carry him over a stretch of water. On the way home he cut through the park and deliberately walked over the park bridge, beneath which ran the boating lake. He thought to himself: "That's fulfilled."

A short while later, circumstances forced a journey to England which he made by sea. Often the things we fear or laugh at have a tendency to come true. The young man found himself seriously considering the fortune-teller's warning. It became a part of him day and night. Pressures of life built up and he felt unable to cope until finally a nervous breakdown followed. Just as the fortune-teller prophesied. When I counselled him he was reasonably well and building up in health again. But great fear gripped his life concerning any relationship with the opposite sex. The third part of the warning nullified any prospect of marriage. For whomever he married would die. I'm glad to say the young man found the elusive peace as he committed his life to Jesus Christ and renounced the visit to the fortune-teller as a work of the devil.

All superstitious and occult practises breed harmful results for the influence penetrates the human mind. Nurturing a fulfillment compulsion. Hitler knew such subjection permitting fear to reign in his life, almost afraid of his own shadow in the quest for destiny.

Against this background, a re-evaluation of the 'halt order' highlights the historians 'dilemma'. The various schools of thought each contain vital truths yet in themselves are not conclusive. The ommission of the King's call to prayer and the presentation of an anonymous Hitler sustain the present ambiguity of thought and unanswered questions. Why? is a question which contains the element of indissoluble problems engulfing the mind.

What then really happened?

Firstly, Hitler's action saved the British Army when nothing else could. Upon this all will agree. Yet the 'halt order' barely lasted forty-eight hours. Just long enough for the British to make their escape to Dunkirk and Hitler to change his mind. How far his mind was changed, no one will ever know. Did he for example still want peace with Britain? The study of a confused man fills the page with question marks.

Confusion! Here lies the answer. God is not limited by time or space. The day the King announced a National Day of Prayer became the day Hitler made his biggest blunder and lost the war. Decision making is never easy, especially when other voices contain the element of suggestion. God answered prayer even before it was made: "before ye call I will answer." Another voice entered the contest for decision, one Hitler did not expect or recognise. Through giving himself over to the prognosticators, firmly believing his horoscope, Hitler felt he couldn't lose yet became confused for the first time regarding military decision.

As discussed in the previous chapter, historians offer various reasons for the 'halt order'. Not one can be dismissed as irrelevant. Unfortunately for Hitler they all became relevant at the same time. Reports underlined the necessity for the tanks receiving maintenance in view of the second phase for the Battle of France; peace with Britain and her Empire would set him up not only as a great military genius but a political giant, the might and power of the Luftwaffe constantly boasted by Goering of capabilities not yet evidenced, together penetrated the thinking of this evil man with the enslaved will.

For once in his life, Hitler obeyed the voice of God, of course unknowingly, as he entered another battle, the one between light and darkness. Between God and the Devil.

"If Dunkirk has any message for us it is the heartening one that Britain will prove to be an impregnable fortress against which Germany's might will be launched in vain. If that attack fails Hitler is lost and all Europe, aye, the whole world is saved. And if Hitler does not venture to attack Britain, he is equally lost."

General Smut's South African Prime Minister.

CHAPTER SIX

The Deliverance

6.57 p.m. Sunday 26th May, 1940 — a time when throughout the British Isles her people crowded the churches of the land — the Admiralty dispatches signalled: 'Operation Dynamo is to Commence'.

Preparatory steps to cover an escape by sea were first taken when an Admiralty order was read out over the B.B.C. following the nine o'clock news on Tuesday 14th May. All owners of self-propelled pleasure craft between thirty and one hundred feet in length were given two weeks in which to forward particulars of their vessels. The response was so magnificent that within a few days the Admiralty built up a register of almost every small craft around the 'isles'. The spirit of the response eulogised by the murmurings of six indignant yachtswomen having their offer rejected.

Admiral Sir Bertram Ramsay, the flag officer commanding Dover, knew only too well enormous difficulties confronted him in the task of the operational planning of 'Dynamo'. Upon his shoulders rested a heavy responsibility, especially in the light of hour by hour reports which suggested the enemy could be expected to be in complete control by the 28th May. Ramsay geared arrangements accordingly in the sincere hope of fulfilling the expectation of lifting between 30-45,000 men from the beaches.

It was a long way from the Isle of Man for steamer *Mona's Isle*. After many years of carrying happy holidaymakers from Liverpool to Douglas (I.O.M.), her new role announced 'Dynamo' operative. She also served to underline a grim message to all who would follow her.

For the sake of speed, Ramsay had sent her across the channel by the shortest possible route. Known as Route Z — a journey of 39 miles from Dover to Dunkirk, the *Mona's Isle* hugged the French coast to within a few miles of Calais. Berthing at Dunkirk shortly after dark she took on 1,420 troops, anxious to get them home to safety. At dawn on the 27th May she sailed by the same route for Dover. The enemy shore batteries between Gravelines and Les Hemmes pounded her. Then the Luftwaffe took over and low-flying Messerschmitts opened up their machine-guns causing death and injury amongst the troops on deck. At Dover, the report of the nightmare journey included the names of twenty-three of her passengers who died during the engagement with the enemy, together with sixty wounded.

Earlier that morning five more transports had made an endeavour to reach Dunkirk. Once again the effective batteries on shore at Gravelines set up a curtain of fire causing the vessels to head back to Dover. Safely, they reached harbour but their empty decks carried an eloquent communique from the enemy. They also helped to destroy the belief that Calais was still holding out. By the time the authorities in London accepted this sad fact, the Germans had enjoyed a full twenty-four hour occupation of the Channel port. Earlier recognition would have saved the R.A.F. many wasted sorties over Calais enabling greater attention to the defence of Dunkirk. Possibly stopping the Luftwaffe making the inner harbour unusable.

The acceptance of the fate of Calais and the German command of the French gun batteries at Gravelines was a death blow to the implementation of Route Z. Fortunately, anticipated planning included two alternative sea lanes: Route Y — now swept for mines approached Dunkirk from the east via Ostend, and Route X joining the Dunkirk Road halfway between Gravelines and Dunkirk. Route X although the next direct route at 55 miles needed several days work to clear the British minefields. Thus the only available route was Route Y. At 87 miles, by far the longest striking the Dunkirk channel near Bray-Dunes after a journey down the Belgian Coast. The disadvantage of this route, although avoiding the shore batteries, exposed the rescue ships to attack by enemy submarines, surface raiders and aircraft. Plus valuable time added to each crossing in a situation becoming all the more delicate as each hour passed. Using Route Y the log of the London tug 'Sun IV' shows a journey time of 8 hours.

From the bridge of the destroyer 'Wolfhound', Captain William Tennant caught his first sight of Dunkirk — his new appointment as Senior Naval Officer in command of Shore Operations. An air-raid was in progress, the town convulsed in flames, over which the sky could not be seen as smoke from the burning oil-refineries rose thousands of feet into the air.

Two hours after arrival, at 8 p.m. on 27th May, Tennant sent off a wire to Admiral Ramsay:

> Please send every available craft to beaches east of Dunkirk immediately. Evacuation tomorrow night is problematical.

The beaches east of Dunkirk, to which Tennant requested the craft to be sent formed the longest continuous expanse of sand in the whole of Europe. Behind the beach lay the sand dunes sprayed with clumps of coarse grass. Together with the dunes, the overall width of the beaches was about one mile. The dunes provided first class assembly areas for troops awaiting embarkation, and for control purposes, the holiday resorts of Malo-les-Bains, Bray Dunes and La Panne were ideally situated. Unfortunately, the characteristic slope along the length of beach could not have had a more untoward design in the consideration of furnishing access for evacuation ships, especially as none of the resorts had a pier.

The men at Dover knew that whilst speed became vital as the enemy closed in, evacuation would be slow and laborious. Not only would the Royal Navy face a complicated task having to navigate in crowded and narrow sea roads, but must operate against a whirlwind opposition. Likewise the Royal Air Force must keep the Luftwaffe somehow at bay. This was 'Miracle' talk in itself.

The first twenty-four hours saw eight and a half thousand British and French troops evacuated from Dunkirk and the beaches. The main difficulty being the frustration of keeping the destroyers waiting a mile off shore for five or six hours whilst the small boats ferried the men. Quickly, Tennant realised Britains hidden fleet of 'small ships' had a vital role to fulfill, so off went the signal to send them all.

At the same time Tennant decided to experiment. The use of Dunkirk's main harbour was out of the question, due to an air-attack seven days previously rendering the harbour unusable. However, two embarkation points were left, a jetty to the west of the harbour and the east mole. Tennant saw the possibilities of the east mole but was not sure in his mind that ships could berth. The only way to find out he used by signalling a ship to try it out. When the *Queen of the Channel* tied up alongside the mole, a new page was added to the Dunkirk epic. Built as a breakwater, entirely made of wood and stretching for 1600 yards, the mole protected the entrance-channel which leads past the lighthouse to the main harbour and docks of the port. Although only five feet across, over two hundred thousand men came home via its sacred planks. Soon the experiment proved it was the easiest place for ships to reach and leave, and in order to speed up the pace of the evacuation, the Navy used it throughout 'Dynamo'. Sixteen ships at one time could berth but not without hazard. Ships were exposed to enemy bombers and shore batteries, as they passed through the narrow entrance, manoeuvered in the outer harbour or lay alongside the mole taking on their precious cargo. The Luftwaffe tried to destroy it as did the German artillery, yet, naked of all defence, the breakwater built to break the force of the waves must have broken many a German bomber pilot's heart. Oftentimes it was hit but gaps in its planked footway were soon repaired. Truly a 'Miracle' in itself and an answer to prayer.

On the afternoon of 29th May, fourteen ships berthed alongside the east mole. In force, the enemy's air armada concentrated a five hour 'blitz'. Before 6 p.m. the harbour scene horrifically exhibited

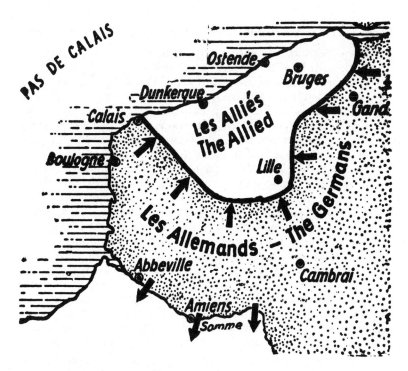

Camarades!

Telle est la situation!
En tout cas, la guerre est finie pour vous!
Vos chefs vont s'enfuir par avion.
A bas les armes!

British Soldiers!

Look at this map: it gives your true situation!
Your troops are entirely surrounded —
stop fighting!
Put down your arms!

German leaflet dropped from the air for the benefit of the British and French troops burning and sinking ships. Veteran, Westby Kirsack, remembers:

I was Second Navigating Officer of *Fenella* when she was sunk with H.M.S. Grenade alongside the east mole at Dunkirk in the early afternoon of 29th May. *Mona's Queen* had been mined in the Eastern Approaches to Dunkirk Port earlier that morning with heavy casualties amongst the crew. Fortunately, she was not loaded with troops at the time. *Fenella* was loading in between the heavy bombing raids and eventually H.M.S. Grenade got a heavy hit amidships and virtually broke in two. *Fenella* got a lighter bomb amidships and a heavy hit in the water right alongside the engine room which ruptured the hull.

Our troops were put back on to the mole along with some captured German Air Force prisoners and re-embarked with *Fenella's* crew on *Crested Eagle*, a former London pleasure paddle steamer in her new sphere of service as a Fleet Air Arm tender. *Crested Eagle* barely got away when she was heavily attacked receiving direct hits on the after deck, where unfortunately the troops plus *Fenella's* crew members were concentrated. *Crested Eagle* was blazing and eventually grounded in the shallow water. Those of us who were not wounded swam ashore to the shelter, relatively speaking, of the sand dunes.

The Isle of Man Steam Packet Company served magnificently but paid dearly. *Fenella*, only built in 1937, now lay in her watery grave. Her sister ship *Tynwald* received high honour for her part in the evacuation, the Captain, Chief Officer and Radio Officer having the Distinguished Service Cross bestowed upon them. Only three years previously it had been such a happy day when launched at Barrow-in-Furness, her graceful lines would certainly enhance the company's fleet causing holidaymakers to feel comfortable in her well fitted compartments. The advent of war altered the whole course of her life but she will be remembered by grateful veterans who found safe refuge within her decks. *Tynwald* survived Dunkirk in order to continue her war career which terminated abruptly in November, 1942 when she was lost in enemy action at Bougie Bay.

Other ships of the Isle of Man Steam Packet Company shared mixed fortunes: *King Orry* received a hit in Dunkirk Roads, settling down in the water almost upright. *Mona's Isle*, as already mentioned, was the first ship to leave Dover on Sunday evening, the 26th May. The damage inflicted by the enemy necessitated her withdrawal from any further part in 'Operation Dynamo'. Much of the evacuation took part at night and the over populated sea lanes faced a new hazard — collision. *Ben-My-Chree* damaged her bows in collision during the darkness and confusion of the night. *Lady of Mann* and *Manxman* survived unscathed.

Isle of Man steamer Mona's Queen built 1934, struck a mine on 29th May 1940 and sank near Port Dunkirk

The Isle of Man ships wrote their names indelibly into the Dunkirk story. Upon them fell the singular honour of being first across to Dunkirk and last back. *Manxman*, the day after the fall of France was the last British vessel to leave the European mainland, lifting General Marshall Cornwall, nearly a thousand British troops and hundreds of Polish and French volunteers.

Today, travellers from Liverpool to Douglas, Isle of Man, in the main are unaware of the vital role played by the company's steamers during those terrifying nine days. Yet their names live on reminding all passengers to be grateful for the 'Miracle of Deliverance'. Perhaps when next sailing on the *Lady of Mann II*, *Mona's Queen V*, *Ben-My-Chree V* or *Manxman II* you will pause awhile in thanksgiving and remembrance.

Westby Kirsack, survivor from the *Fenella*, after the war became the company's Marine Superintendent. Today, he is a minister in the Church of England but above all a Dunkirk Veteran:

> I hope to return in service to God some of the love which has come to me.

During the latter part of May, the populace of Dover and other south coast ports became aware that Allied forces were in a far more serious situation than most Britons realised. Daily at Dover in particular, the build up of batches of wounded arriving in naval ships caused the townspeople to ponder and openly ask: "Is this defeat?" When vessels of every sort began to arrive from Dunkirk the people had little time to give to such a serious question for there was so much to do. Mr. F. Pascall of Dover remembers:

> On the morning of this daring rescue of our beleaguered forces from the beaches, it was unduly mild, following some very inclement weather, and it was a most extraordinary sight to see hundreds of boats of almost every kind stretched out over Dover harbour and beyond. At the time, only those immediately involved knew the meaning of the vast fleet at anchor. The wonderful rescue was without doubt one of the most brave and daring in our history.
>
> Later that day and onwards, it was very evident these small ships, with entire disregard for their own safety were bringing back every possible man. The wounded were taken to local hospitals, trains took the bulk of the survivors inland. The casualties were taken to the main hospital in Union Road (now named Coombe Valley Road) in every available vehicle. Due to the large numbers of wounded they were laid in rows on the floor, awaiting treatment.

> Mr. John Husk, a local haulage contractor with premises and yard in the road was asked to provide as many helpers as possible to assist at the hospital. Especially, the few men available

for stretcher work. John, known with affection as the 'Father' of the district because of his ever willing hand extended to those in need, soon had a willing band of helpers in action. I was one of John's helpers for several nights and was amazed at the wonderful work undertaken by the doctors and nurses. It seemed they were endowed with extra strength. In particular Dr. Gertrude Toland and her staff in the operating theatre as they toiled unceasingly. As a very humble, and sometimes frightened onlooker, it surprised me that this wonderful 'Scots' lady was never included in the list of appreciative awards issued, whilst decorations were given to local persons with mundane jobs.

Fighter cover for 'Dynamo' was provided by Air Vice-Marshal Park on lines laid down by Air Chief Marshal Dowding. During the evacuation the Royal Air Force averaged 300 sorties a day over Dunkirk. Losses proved heavy with 177 aircraft destroyed or severely damaged, eighty pilots losing their lives. There is no means of telling how many German aircraft they destroyed, but it would appear safe to credit them with most of the 132 known to have been lost by the Luftwaffe at Dunkirk or in unspecified areas. Whilst statistics are necessary they tend to become cold and unyielding when faced with the true state of affairs. Perhaps the testimony of a German pilot captured at Dunkirk reveals how they became the cavalry of the clouds fighting out the eternal combat between light and darkness; between right and wrong:

> Your pilots are not men, they are fanatics. They are some new kind of devil. They came at us like the furies of hell. It did not matter how strong we were, they went for us as if we were sheep and they fought us at any odds. Our orders were to reach Dunkirk and bomb the British Army and Navy out of existence, but your mad pilots turned the skies into a madhouse.

On the British side, an officer of high rank declared:

> These fellows who come to us in this war are different from any I have seen before. The only way I can describe it is that they are men with a mission. There is something going on inside their souls that is a closed book to those of us who belong to an older generation. They are not cruel, but they are relentless. They seem to see in the German Air Force the absolute expression of the scientific domination which Hitler would enforce on the world if he can win. These chaps fight as if it were not a war at all, but a crusade. They look up at the skies as if they have been called up to cleanse them of something vile and obscene. And they simply do not believe in the possibility of defeat.

Again the weather befriended the Crusaders of land, sea and air. Following the massive raid of 27th May — when the Luftwaffe carried out twelve major attacks on Dunkirk, using a total of 300 bombers, the twenty-eighth started overcast. As the day progressed the weather worsened, severely spoiling Luftwaffe operations. Next morning, pouring rain and low cloud formations inflicted further set backs in the enemy camp, frustrating their eagerness to attack the ships and boats now stealing their prey as they twiddled their thumbs. By mid-day on the twenty-ninth the clouds broke up enabling the enemy to resume dive-bombing operations. However, suitable conditions deteriorated once more and 30th May announced itself with fog and rain. Anxiously, German bomber crews stood at the ready awaiting orders which could not be issued until early afternoon on the thirty-first. True to its designation the Glorious First of June presented a sunny and clear day which the Luftwaffe welcomed. It was a day of severe conflict and losses on both sides. Four destroyers plus ten other craft died as dive-bombers discharged their lethal cargo. By the end of the day Fighter Command counted 31 aircraft lost. German losses remain in doubt due to conflicting reports. Luftwaffe records admit 29 destroyed with 13 damaged. Fighter Command claimed 78 enemy aircraft shot down but later officially reduced to 43, the Royal Navy claimed 10 enemy aircraft coupled with a similar claim by the French fighters.

What is not in doubt is that on 1st June over 64,000 men were brought home. The weather aiding the allies but restricting the enemy brought about the 'Miracle of Deliverance'. Here, in a department beyond the control of man, God arranged in response to believing prayer, inclement conditions for the sky vikings and a mill-pond channel to favour the smallest of ships. A factor causing countless skippers of small boats to take the decision in carrying double their normal passenger compliment. The following figures tell their own story:

NUMBERS OF BRITISH AND ALLIED FORCES BROUGHT TO ENGLAND

Date of arrival	Total men	From Dunkirk	From beaches	Weather Comments
May 27	7,669	7,669	—	Heavy enemy bombing raid
May 28	17,804	11,874	5,930	Enemy aircraft grounded due to weather
May 29	47,310	33,558	13,752	Enemy aircraft grounded until early afternoon
May 30	53,823	24,311	29,512	Enemy aircraft grounded all day
May 31	68,014	45,072	22,942	Enemy aircraft grounded until early afternoon

H.M.S. Venetia one of the rescue ships at Boulogne. Pictured when the author's father served in her

June 1	64,429	47,081	17,348	Heavy bombing raid and sky battle
June 2	26,256	19,561	6,695	Reduced bomber activity
June 3	26,746	26,746	—	120 bomber raid broken up by R.A.F. little damage
June 4	26,175	26,175	—	
Totals for Dynamo	338,226	242,047	96,179	

The English Channel ports from Dover to Margate had never witnessed anything like it before. Vessels of every description greeted the first light and the awakening populance. Jannette and Alison Bark of Broadstairs preserve the sight fresh in their minds:

> The sea had been like a mill-pond with gloriously warm days as can only be experienced in this corner of the British Isles. The disturbing worries being the pall of gunsmoke across the twenty-one mile stretch of the English Channel coupled with the incessant noise of heavy guns which shook the plate-glass windows of all the shops.
>
> Living on the front at Broadstairs we saw the Armada begin to grow. Each morning as the sun rose we looked out to see each day more boats either motorised or just small rowing boats. They were in perfect formation and the lines of the motor yacht did not look out of place beside the rowing boat. In the end they stretched from the Thames estuary round the coast as far as we could see.
>
> At the time I was working in a grocery store and the first intimation we had that the operation had really started being when one of our customers from North Foreland came in and asked what we could spare for her to take to Ramsgate Harbour. Our manager telephoned Head Office with the news, receiving orders to, 'send everything you have that is needed'. Never were costly cars so quickly loaded with tea, sugar, biscuits, cakes, bovril, oxo, cocoa, butter and margarine. It must be remembered these were mainly rations for the remaining civilians. Red-Cross vans, buses, various voluntary organisations and churches of all denominations concentrated at the various harbours, occupying any available building in setting up their tea urns and sandwich trays.
>
> We had a Scotsman of considerable wealth living at St. Augustines, the home of the late Frederick Morgan the artist. This Mr. Stuart usually did not waste words but acted quickly. At this crucial time he bought every blanket from the town's shops for delivery to Margate and Ramsgate.

Then there was the Boatman who in happier days employed his small rowing boat for trips in the bay. He had just received news that his son had been killed in action, yet still he carried on using his boat calling out, 'any more for a trip across the bay.'

At Dover, Ramsgate, Margate; wherever the little ships found safe haven the scene of willing helpers was constant. Many decks became hazardous to helpers encountering difficulty in keeping their feet because everywhere was so slippery with blood. It became a familiar sight as seamen took hoses to wash down the decks and play the hoses over the ship's side where blood had run through the scuppers.

Major Paul, Adjutant of the Royal Army Service Corps depot at Connaught Barracks, Woolwich, was taken aback when by telephone he received a request for 200 men to undertake an urgent job. Being informed the name of the exercise — 'Dynamo'. Manpower being what it was at the time causing the major to indicate a promise of between 20-40 men. In response to obvious questions the major put the telephone down with the following picture of the exercise to begin:—

(a) To open up buffets at Paddock Wood, Taversham and Chichester railway stations with the object of feeding troops passing through. When the train moves out prepare for the next and report numbers.

(b) Number to be fed — uncertain. At least 5,000 and possibly 10,000. Over a period of just a couple of days.

(c) Men on light duty plus those standing by to be used plus anyone else you can find.

(d) At each station one officer will be in charge assisted by a sergeant, two or three corporals and what men you can muster. SUPPLIES:— bread, meat, rolls, cheese, tea, sugar, milk.

Major Paul called his staff to a conference in his office explaining the operation as urgent and implementing immediate arrangements for the supply of vehicles, trestle top tables, cooking stoves, utensils, mugs, knives, blankets and food.

Naturally the major was asked what it was all about, to which he replied: "I've no idea, all I've been told is we've to feed 5,000, possibly 10,000 troops. I suspect they are mostly colonial, coming up to man coast defences from Salisbury Plain and district." Major Paul reported to Eastern Command that stations had been manned and for the next 24 hours all was quiet. Later the next day the officer in charge at Paddock Wood, rang up: "We've had our first train through but it's going the other way."

Major Paul then knew how all his thinking had been so wrong. So good had been security that although laying on the exercise he had no idea what it was for. This made all the difference for he now wanted to know what the men from Dunkirk wanted rather than what he would supply. Soon he knew. The first thing these fellows asked for was a good cup of tea. They didn't go much for bully beef, meat loaf, biscuits but the things they hadn't seen for a bit: sausages, eggs, fruit, cakes and cigarettes. After consultation with Eastern Command, the major had a free hand to supply the men with anything they wanted.

The workers from the sausage factory didn't expect to receive a 7 ton order, with more to follow whilst relaxing on their annual outing to a London theatre. Immediately they vacated their seats to return to the factory and get on with the job. An officer detailed for the strangest mission of his military career, cornered the banana market at Covent Garden. Now the menu started to take on a more varied appearance.

The original intimation of a two or three day exercise stretched into a week and still the trains rolled up. Some carried German Prisoners who were astonished at being treated without discrimination. From an initial estimate of 5,000 which in itself did not give much hope of survival, the 200,000 total was chalked up. Approaching 300,000 the frequency of trains slackened and no one needed any official pronouncement to indicate the end was in sight. In the last trains came the padres, medical staffs with a greater proportion of officers. Finally, the stations were quiet — it was over. Another miracle had taken place by feeding sixty times as many as originally expected.

Carnage! A sad and yet apt word to describe the scene off the beaches of Dunkirk. The sea appeared to be strayed with blazing ships not exactly a heartening welcome to the rescue armada. But the sight of the thousands of men on the beaches stirred the trawlers, cockle boats, tugs, drifters, barges, schuyts, pleasure boats, as well as the destroyers and minesweepers, to press on regardless. Braving the enemy dive bombers with the hidden menace of mines. Many never made it; some like the herring drifter, *Silver Dawn* could only complete one trip due to striking obstacles in the harbour of Dunkirk. Even so, little drifters under orders to limit their human cargo to about 100 men would roll up in England with 250 men aboard, thanks to nature's gift of a calm sea. Another herring boat, *Fisher Boy* managed seven trips lifting 1,350 men.

Much of the evacuation took place at night. Such course of action reducing dangers from the enemy experienced during daylight. But new difficulties confronted the tense and tired seamen delicately manipulating their craft through overcrowded sea lanes in pitch darkness. *Arctic Pioneer*, fired upon an R.A.F. launch, supposing her to be a German 'E' Boat. Stopping to pick up surviv-

Top: The Germans move into the 'Dunes'
Bottom: French soldiers captured at Dunkirk

ors, her crew felt great remorse in the realisation of a tragic and terrible mistake. This fishing trawler had landed some strange fish in her time but none more peculiar when out of the sea they fished a Frenchman clad in steel helmet, great coat, bandolier and field boots.

The drifter, *Comfort*, en route for La Panne, stopped to pick up and search for the few survivors from the destroyer *Wakeful* which had been torpedoed. Most of her 650 troops aboard, asleep below decks, went down with the ship broken in two by the explosion and sinking in seconds. The destroyer *Grafton* and the drifter *Lydd* both laden with troops on the way back to England, joined the rescue. Other vessels in the vicinity closed in to render whatever help possible Lifeboats from the *Comfort*, minesweeper *Lydd*, drifter *Nautilus* and *Grafton*, frantically searched for what was left of *Wakeful's* crew. *Grafton's* captain, thinking the unlighted vessel about a thousand yards away to be another drifter, sent out a signal to join the search. Seconds later, torpedoes from 'U' 69 blew the destroyer apart.

The assisting vessels sailed away in all directions and what followed is the saddest of all Dunkirk stories. The captain of the minesweeper *Lydd*, spotted what appeared to be an enemy torpedo boat. He engaged the enemy by opening fire. Although sinking, the *Grafton* lined her guns on the dimly lit vessel. *Lydd* set a ramming course and minutes later her bow sliced into the vessel's hull, splitting her in two. In the confusion of the darkness a fearful tragedy had been enacted: for the victim of *Grafton* and *Lydd* was no enemy torpedo boat. She was the drifter *Comfort* carrying survivors from the destroyer *Wakeful*. There were few survivors from *Comfort*.

Nevertheless, the most fantastic fleet ever put out from the shores of England continued to bob its way across the channel. Finding, upon arrival men queuing up in lines stretching out into the sea. Some ankle-deep, others knee-deep, many in water up to their chins before the little boats picked them up. Veteran J. Newbold of Grimsby couldn't swim but with water bobbing around his head and the rescue ship a few feet away, he decided this was the time to learn — to save his life. Around them, caught in the ebb and flow of tide floated their own dead comrades either killed by enemy gun-fire or drowned in the sinking of rescue ships. A corps commander said:

> I have had opportunities of witnessing British soldiers over a large number of years, both in war and peace and I have never seen them behave in a more exemplary manner.

An American newspaper reporter, at that time representing a neutral country, wired his editor:

These soldiers had what it took. They kept their heads and hearts, and their heads and hearts kept them. There's no truer test of greatness in a man or an army than the test of adversity.

The rescue ships found jutting out into the sea improvised piers made of army lorries with a plank walk on top to facilitate the embarkation of waiting troops. Veteran Charles Stewart of Rowlands Castle, Hants., helped to build such a pier. He recalls:

A Royal Marine Officer took charge of us — sixteen sappers on the beach at La Panne. It all started with an overloaded rowing boat, its keel stuck in the sand, and no-one was getting anywhere. A unit pal and I stepped out of the boat, pushing and heaving until it floated. Unfortunately, we were left behind.

Arriving back on the beach our troubles began. We were promptly collared by this officer, who had us strapping lorries together to form a Pier out to sea whilst he kept darting off, bringing back an odd sapper or two. Don't ask me where or how, but suddenly a sixteen-handled paddle-boat appeared, and three of us were detailed to guard this boat with orders to shoot anyone rash enough to take it. He found his Sappers, also some rum, then loading this paddle-boat we pushed out to sea to the rescue ship. What a man! I do not recall him even repeating himself. We humble sappers were the cause of the plight you all found yourselves in. We were the cause of Hitler himself. Now he carried on! "Row you shower, row."

I cannot recall the number of trips made, or at least by this time did not care with this type of officer. I seemed to think he could snatch any one of the stukers diving at us, and pull it to pieces. Naturally he achieved his object — the angrier he made us the more we took it out of the paddle. There was no hint at all when the final trip would come. When it did, what a change in his manner. We were not to blame after all, instead we became the salt of the earth — almost the saviour of dear old England itself.

I will remember his words to the chaps we had rowed over: 'These sappers have worked hard for you', and calling out to Jack aboard the *Worcester*, 'look after them they have done a great job.' The last I saw of him was detailing sixteen passengers to take over, knowing they would take the blame for all that happened.

As the enemy drew closer raining heavy shelling upon the beaches and Dunkirk channel, somehow, despite it all the rescue vessels, British strange armada, plied back and forth through the barrier of death. Somehow, despite it all the important East Mole, under perpetual attack from land and air, miraculously still stood.

Somehow, despite it all, Dunkirk harbour and its approaches, housing countless wrecks, polluted with oil and debris plus the grim sight of floating bodies was still usable.

Soon the end would come. Feverishly, with disregard for self-preservation, sailors from British destroyers went into the burning town searching for scattered survivors. One naval officer staged an unusual sight of marching through the burning streets playing bagpipes to rally stragglers from the many cellars. In the cellar of a hotel they found the Mayor of Dunkirk in full regalia surrounded by frightened women and children, together with British soldiers awaiting the arrival of the Germans.

On the morning of 3rd June, General Alexander toured the beaches; satisfied that all B.E.F. men were away he ordered Captain Tennant to join him aboard the departing destroyer. Finally, at 2.23 p.m. on 4th June the British and French Commanders agreed that Operation Dynamo should be ended.

As H.M.S. Shikari, laden with French soldiers and bearing scars of battle wrote her name in history as the last ship to leave the battered harbour, German tanks entered as victors . . . unaware that through the prayers of British people the Hand of God had wrought on their behalf 'A Miracle of Deliverance'.

At Dunkirk, Germany lost the war through the hesitations of Hitler. From Dunkirk an army came home — was re-equipped — and out of the ranks of these 'delivered' men arose future household names like Montgomery — Alexander.

> So long as the English tongue survives, the word Dunkirk will be spoken with reverence. In that harbour — such a hell as never blazed on earth before — at the end of a lost battle the rags and blemishes that had hidden the soul of democracy fell away. There, beaten but unconquered, in shining splendour, she faced the enemy, this shining thing in the souls of free men which Hitler cannot command. It is the great tradition of democracy. It is the future. It is victory.
>
> New York Times
> 1st June, 1940.

LA PANNE . . . . the jetty constructed of abandoned vehicles overlaid with planks was the brainchild of Lt. Colonel Harold Dibbens (then Lieutenant) Military Police. Although the sea remained calm throughout the evacuation there was however, a slight swell on the morning of Thursday, 30th May. Due to haste and poor seamanship, dinghies were capsizing and drifting away. Veteran Dibbens recalls: "It then struck me that if a jetty could be erected we could bring the boats alongside and load them more efficiently and with comparative safety. My mind almost at once

Dunkirk ablaze and German soldiers arriving in Dunkirk

turned to the heavy lorries standing around which I felt could be used to form a base for a pier . . . I found a Royal Engineer captain and told him what was going through my mind. I also mentioned that my military police would provide the vehicles and if he would work with me and his men would be the first troops to embark via the jetty." This inspiring moment in the life of Veteran Dibbens bore much fruit as many thousands walked his pier to safety. He also experienced something very personal: "When I was within sight of the sea something told me I had nothing to fear."

Dunkirk today, at low tide the sea uncovers wrecks as a grim reminder

CHAPTER SEVEN

A Church on the Dunes

During Roman times, the Dunkirk area as we know it today, was under water, a consequence of the great flood of the 4th century. When the area began to dry up the waters deposited lime and sand in the stiller waters and a small rise of land gave birth to a range of dunes along the coast.

As higher lands emerged, the Romans busied themselves in building dykes and fishermen settled on the higher ground sheltered from the sea. During the 7th century, the fishermen received a visit from St. Eloi who brought the Christian message. Dunkirk received its name when St. Eloi built a church on the dunes: Dun = dunes, kirk = church. Around which the town grew.

Historically, Dunkirk presents many upheavals. It came under the domination of the Courts of Flanders and was successfully ruled by Burgundy, Austria and Spain. As the first local historian Faulconnier wrote: "Our town changed hands three times in one day, each time being taken over by one of the most powerful European nations. It was Spanish in the morning, French at lunchtime and English in the evening, due to a treaty signed by France and England." Bought back by Louis XIV from the English, Dunkirk became French in 1662.

The seaside, between the port and the town of Leffrinckoucke is a long stretch of fine sand. On a cold but calm winter's morning I walked along the tiled promenade from Malo-les-Bains, taking in the slow rising tide which only covers part of the sand; restaurants; hotels and of course the long stretch of dunes. Very few people were about — it seemed so peaceful. Yet it was here, 'a miracle of deliverance' took place.

At the west end of the beach lies the Memorial dedicated to the Allied Soldiers who lost their lives during the battles of May — June, 1940. After a few photographs, I paused to say a humble, 'Thank You'. I began to think, "little did St. Eloi realise it would become a Church on the Dunes far surpassing any of his dreams." The old building may have long since been demolished but in May, 1940 the whole area became 'A Church on the Dunes' to the British Expeditionary Force housed beneath the care of the protecting Hand of God.

Veteran John Davies of Poole, Dorset made it his church. Upon the outbreak of war, a regular soldier serving with the South Lancashire Regiment, he was sent to France. Whilst the unit made its way to the beaches he was detailed to form the rearguard at Nieuport with orders to hold the position for four hours. Generous supplies of ammunition together with a review of the seriousness of the situation prompted sobering reactions; John recognised the responsibility and adherence to orders placed a heavy burden upon him. Experienced men were worth their weight in gold — they were looked up to — counted as reliable.

Watching his unit pull out and head for Dunkirk, he longed to be going with them. "Are we to be sacrificed?" he questioned within himself. "Is this where I die?" ran through his mind. Obedience! For a soldier simply a part of life with penalties if one fails to comply. The men set to work in preparing defences and tactics designed to delude the Germans into thinking they were facing the crack 4th Division. Every man knew how vital the role of the next four hours, especially John Davies. The uncertainty of living through the next few hours weighed heavily in his troubled mind. "After death the judgement!" Words from the Bible, read and heard so many times when a member of the Salvation Army. Words he knew not only to be true but ones which struck terror far deeper than the immediate German threat. For six years he had cast aside the godly living and example he had shown. But now the voice of God could be heard once again. John fell to his knees making fresh vows to serve God afresh if only He would get him home safely.

When the time came for John and his men to pull out he recalls: "The Lord answered my prayers, as the party I led made our way to the beaches it seemed as though The Lord was the leader. Although we had a lot to contend with and lost some men, we arrived back in England safe."

Back in England John continued to live as previously: "How fickle we are, I never kept my part of the bargain until late 1940, when I made the final decision at Parkstone, Poole where I now live. I accepted Christ once again as my Saviour and Friend."

Now he was a soldier in two armies with new found Christian comrades. His Christian friends made a promise to constantly pray for him as John fought the enemy in various theatres of war, including being one of the first to land in France in the 'D' Day invasion.

When we reformed after Dunkirk, we were placed in the crack 3rd Division, I seemed to bear a charmed life for whatever attack I was in, I survived; and I believe that it was through the prayers of the Christian friends that I made, when I started to serve my Lord afresh, that I am here today.

In 1946 John began to play in the local Salvation Army Band —
today he's still playing away. With pride he belongs to another
army — The Dunkirk Veterans Association; remembering when
those sands became his 'Church on the Dunes'.

The sight of men sleeping the sleep of exhaustion in the sand
hills; the pale sand disfigured by abandoned equipment and blanket covered bodies of comrades killed on the beach played heavily
upon the mind of Veteran Cyril Best. Three days on the beach
seemed an eternity, now he wondered what came next as he
entered into that loneliness which is beyond human description:

> When my need was greatest; the help came in a mysterious
> way; but it came and I shall never forget it.
>
> There had been three of us, all friends from the same unit who
> had stuck together when the Staff-Sergeant issued orders to
> make our own way to St. Martins Quay. During a Stuka raid
> we became separated.
>
> Alone I wandered, eventually finding myself on Bray Dunes. I
> was very tired, thirsty and hungry. Fire had prevented me
> from approaching the quay, and cut me off from any hope of
> evacuation.
>
> In Dunkirk and on the beaches there was chaos, the oil tanks
> were on fire and a pall of smoke stretched out across the sky.
> Lost — no information as to the location of the enemy — no
> idea as to how I was to escape — my morale couldn't have been
> lower. I had seen my best friend killed, now he lay with the
> silent army strewn along the beach. Constantly I scanned the
> horizon for sighting of a rescue ship, each glance added disap-
> pointment upon disappointment until I gave away my last
> particle of hope.
>
> When night fell I made my way on to the top of Bray Dunes in
> search of cover and somewhere to sleep.
>
> Back came the Luftwaffe dropping magnesium flares produ-
> cing a light as bright as day. From nowhere a voice shouted
> "get down or I'll shoot you!" Like a flash I was flat on my face
> crawling towards a sand-bagged pit spotted during the demon-
> stration of German illuminations. When I pitched in head
> first I became deaf to the abuse as gratefully I found a space to
> crouch down.
>
> Out of the darkness a fellow on my left spoke to me. I had no
> idea who he was and my reply couldn't have helped him very
> much. He must have sensed I was in despair for he said,
> "Cheer up old chap, we'll get away." All the time he led the
> conversation, never once making any reference to himself,
> rather directing attention to myself and my home. Suddenly
> my despair seemed to vanish, I can't explain it but from that
> moment fear and trembling vanished. I had hope and I just

71

knew I would get back to England. I have never felt so up-lifted in my life.

We must have talked for half-an-hour and I still had no idea what my new friend looked like. It was then he mentioned he knew someone who was an Engineer Officer who should be down on the beach organising something. Intimating his intention to find this person and bring back any information, as he clambered up he asked me if I would look after 'his things'.

Into my care he placed a water bottle, a roll of papers and his cap. "Back soon!" he said.

By first light he hand't returned. I looked at the roll of papers in my hand which upon examination turned out to be, "The War Diary of the 22nd Casualty Clearing Station R.A.M.C." Turning to his cap it is that which has indeliably imprinted my experience for all time. The cap badge bore the 'sign of the cross with the words around, "Through His Cross We Conquer". The belongings were those of a holy man and there is no doubt a third person in the form of God had been with us both that night.

I never heard of him again but only hope he got back home safely to do for others what he did for me."

Cyril Best not only survived but went on to see service in West Africa, Burma and India. Promotion followed and at the end of the war he returned home with the rank of Captain.

Today he lives in Cheltenham but cannot forget the night those sands became his "Church on the Dunes".

On Sunday, 26th May, St. Peter's Church in pleasant Parkstone, Dorset, was crowded to the door for the evening service. Ten year old London evacuee Richard Black looked around the large con-gregation gathered in response to the King's call to pray, "What a lot of people", he thought.

Veteran John Wyllie was thinking the same thing at the same time as he gathered around the Army Padre in the dunes at La Panne. Dishevelled, exhausted men bowed their heads in prayer, sharing with the Padre a prayer for deliverance. As a driver with the R.A.S.C. he had driven through numerous air-attacks on the way to La Panne.

We were being bombed and machine-gunned and many of the houses were reduced to rubble. I had to stop in order to clean part of the road and as I returned to the vehicle a house in front of me had its whole face blown away. On the back wall of the room the only thing left hanging was the half life size figure of Christ on the Cross. To me it seemed alive — I couldn't forget it.

72

As John closed his eyes he thought of the many comrades unable to participate in this sacred moment. Pals lying in grotesque attitudes of death, mouths open wide covered in blood and their own inners. It was difficult to believe that only a short while before he had joked with them, exchanged personal intimacies. Now this hallowed spot became his 'Church on the Dunes'.

> I was only half-alive and everything was so faint. But thanks to God I am here today.

Meanwhile, further along the beach, Veteran Harry Pickett stood in the freshly dug hole in the sands with head bowed in prayer. Together with others he testified that during the service he experienced the power of the Spirit of God come upon his life. Some fellow comrades of the 6th Battalion The Royal Lincolnshire Regiment spoke of seeing a group of Angels hovering over them.

A regular soldier, Veteran Harry Smith hated church parade and would do anything else if he could miss the event. Today, he is a different man:

> I have had a very hard life but I thank God for it because I was allowed by Him to live — to love and to be His servant.

Dunkirk changed everything for Harry when unknown to him at the time it became 'The House of God'. "Yes! Dunkirk converted me", he testifies. The sight of men praying on their hands and knees brought this conviction to his heart "that the Lord does help every one — even the worst of sinners."

Later in the war, Harry was captured by the Germans and sent to a prisoner-of-war camp. Now he carried a Bible. On the inside cover it bore:—

A Message From His Majesty The King

> To all serving in my Forces by sea or land, or in the air, and indeed, to all my people engaged in the defence of the Realm, I commend the reading of this book. For centuries the Bible has been a wholesome and strengthening influence in our national life, and it behoves us in these momentous days to turn with renewed faith to this Divine source of comfort and inspiration.

During a private devotional time he read: "They that sow in tears shall reap in joy." Through reading and prayer, 'inspiration' for a plan of escape took root. Deliberation gave way to action, "and I escaped with God's help."

Extracts from an article by C.B. Mortlock in the Daily Telegraph of 8th June, 1940 indicate striking testimony to 'A Church on the Dunes'.

Chaplains have remarked on another circumstance that seemed almost miraculous — the strange immunity by which the troops at times were favoured. One of them told me, for instance, how he lay down with 400 men who were machine-gunned systematically, up and down, and bombed by about 60 enemy aircraft, and in the end there was not a single casualty. Another chaplain was likewise machine-gunned and bombed as he lay on the beach, and when, after what seemed an eternity, he realised he had not been hit, he rose to find that the sand all round where he had lain was pitted with bullet holes and that his figure was thus outlined on the ground.

An ambulance driver told me a most unusual story:—

On one trip, near the end, my driver was killed so I brought the ambulance back to base. As there were no spare drivers I drove it up the line again. On the way I was hit and I had to rip off my blazing uniform. Nearby was the body of a dead Frenchman. Clad in his uniform, I returned to St. Valery using a deserted Bedford truck and continued to load the wounded onto the ships. Several times I felt sorely tempted to remain on the ships. However, sense of duty, or some guiding hand prevailed. It was fortunate for me, and sad to see two of the ships sunk before they had gone far.

I was taken prisoner, and as I could speak French and a little German, being the only medical orderly I was left behind with around 400 wounded. All British officers and men were marched off to Poland.

Helping to transport the wounded to Rouen, I worked on the wards of a hospital assisting the British doctors. Much of my work lay in the area of an interpreter for the Germans and the French. Because of my uniform I was taken as a Frenchman gaining the advantage of being allowed into the town centre and meeting people who would give me chocolate, cigarettes etc., which I passed on to the patients. The big disadvantage being I could not write home — the Germans said the only permissible letters allowed addressed to my next-of-kin, who, according to them must be French. As I had been reported missing, then missing believed killed, it was rough on my mother and sisters. Christmas Day 1941 changed everything for them when a letter I had managed to smuggle by civilians, through France, Spain and Gibralter, arrived as an unexpected Christmas present.

In the early days of captivity we had no Padres, so I did what I could utilising the experience gained as an officer in the Boys Brigade of my local Church at home where often I took the Bible Class.

I was soon to discover the men felt at ease when I was praying,

74

Top: Allied equipment abandoned at Dunkirk
Bottom: British troops heading for an evacuation point

conducting a funeral, or giving a discourse on a Bible subject applicable to prevailing circumstances. This continued throughout prison days and even when moved to bigger camps housing several Padres, the barrackroom service was much better attended, mainly through the advantage of living with the men.

On one journey to another camp we were shipped by train in horse boxes. Each box contained 75 men and the journey lasted 4 days in severe winter conditions. Communication between the men presented natural difficulties due to the nationalities represented. Soldiers from France, Belgium, Poland and Serbia made up the party.

After prayer, I was given the Gift of Tongues to conduct a simple service for each group in their own language. An Act of God, for I didn't know any Polish or Serb. There was a much greater tolerance of each other in these terrible conditions and we shared what we had. As an N.C.O. I was issued with the rations for 10 men, the four day store consisting of one loaf and a large bottle of water. The gospel story of 'the miracle of the feeding of the five thousand' took a new setting.''

It will come as no surprise to learn that today this veteran serves as a humble Christian Minister. Returning home shortly before the end of the war he was posted to a hospital where he met a young woman whom he married. It was wonderful to be alive; free and able to face the future with a new determination. The birth of a son brought much joy and blessing into their home — the war — suffering — five lost years of freedom quickly sped into the dim past ages of antiquity. Life had begun anew.

The announcement of a second addition to the family heralded delight but opened the page to commence a new chapter in the life of this veteran.

My wife was seriously ill so I left my job to look after our young son, working only in the evenings for an Insurance Company. She fought for her life, and doctors were only waiting for her strength to be sufficient to operate and remove the baby. However, as weeks turned into months they decided otherwise and a normal birth took place. Three weeks later our new daughter was baptised. But on the following Wednesday I contracted Polio and spent the next 18 months in a plaster cast only able to move my right arm. The prediction of the doctors brought the bad news that never would I be able to walk again. As if enough of my life had been wasted. I left school at 13½ — my mother was a first war widow. Regarding education — in the main I was self-taught. Whilst in such condition, my wife and local minister received a shock when I declared my intention to become a Christian Minister. I studied Latin,

Greek, English and polished up my French and German. Examination success followed and I gained a university place.

During the next two years, my health improved beyond the expectation of the medical experts, though I always determined to walk again. The day came when I walked out of hospital, not without struggle, clad in calipers. After a few weeks at home, I cut one caliper off, a month later removing the other. For the second time in my life I had to learn how to walk. At first I couldn't use crutches due to paralysis in one arm. Thankfully this condition improved and I was off under my own steam.

Obtaining an old bicycle I fitted it with a very low gear attaching a strap to keep my weaker foot fixed to the pedal, thus forcing my leg to bend up and down. Strength returned.

Today I can get around for distances up to about one mile.

It is now twenty years since this brave and determined veteran received Holy Orders yet he will never forget the day Dunkirk became his 'Church on the Dunes':

I would suggest that Dunkirk, St. Valery and other prisoner-or-war camps were not trials of my weakness of faith, but stimuli towards the build up of faith to face whatever should follow, as God will never put a burden upon us which we cannot bear with His help — only when we try to 'go it alone' do we suffer.

Winston Churchill referred to "a miracle of deliverance, achieved by valour, by perseverance, by perfect discipline, by faultless service, by resource, by skill, by unconquerable fidelity." But even so, this deliverance only became possible when Dunkirk — 'A Church on the Dunes' reverberated with the Divine Presence. Now a church is a place where we enter to worship and leave to witness. Dunkirk is not one story — but a thousand or more.

Shortly after the evacuation, as if Divinely guided, C.B. Mortlock writing in the Daily Telegraph sensed that the Dunkirk story unfolded an unusual element:

As the story is told, two great wonders stand forth; and on them have turned the fortune of the troops. I have talked to officers and men who have got safely back to England, and all of them tell of these two phenomena. The first was the great storm which broke over Flanders on Tuesday 28th May, and the other the great calm which settled on the English Channel during the following days.

Officers of high rank do not hesitate to put down the deliverance of the B.E.F. to the fact of the nation being at prayer on Sunday 26th May. . . . The consciousness of miraculous deliverance pervades the camps in which the troops are now

77

housed in England. An instance of that occurred soon after a large camp had been more or less improvised, and many willing helpers were rivalling each other in giving comfort, refreshment and entertainment to the men. Among other arrangements was an E.N.S.A. concert, and, in the midst of it, at the request of the men, the chaplain conducted an act of thanksgiving consisting of a hymn and prayers and a few simple words.

One Chaplain told me that he was in a party who were taken aboard a minesweeper. They were all drenched to the skin, having been up to the shoulders in water. On deck it was impossible for anybody to stand. Presently there was a call for the padre to say a prayer. With the help of men on either side of him and behind him, the chaplain got up and the whole of the bedraggled ship's company joined with him in offering thanksgiving to God for their wonderful deliverance.

The story of the strange armada which took the men from the beaches of Dunkirk is already familiar in outline. In its complete fullness it will probably never be known, but it is undoubted that there was such a calmness over the whole of the waters of the English Channel for that vital period of days as has rarely been experienced. Those who are accustomed to the Channel testify to the strangeness of this calm, they are deeply impressed by the phenomenon of nature by which it became possible for the tiny craft to go back and forth in safety.

So the two miracles made possible what seemed impossible. In the darkness of the storm and the violence of the rain, formations which were eight to twelve miles from Dunkirk were able to move up on foot to the coast with scarcely any interruption from aircraft, for aircraft were unable to operate in such turbulent conditions!

Veteran Charles Wilson, 1st Battalion Royal Hampshire Regiment pinpoints his deliverance to the storm. He recalls:—

Our unit was being shot up by the German Air Force, when suddenly dark clouds came over, and a thunderstorm broke. Jerry left us and a voice called out, 'God is protecting us.' We marched on feeling a lot better but soaked through.

Wherever you find a 'Dunkirk Veteran' you will find a grateful man. The following anonymous poem caught up by the wind found its way into a slit trench at El Aghelia during a very heavy bombardment:

A SOLDIER — HIS PRAYER

Stay with me God, the night is dark,
The night is cold, my little spark of courage dies,

The night is long, Be with me God and make me strong.

You stilled the waters at Dunkirk
And saved your servants, All your work is wonderful, dear
God,
You strode before us down that dreadful road.
We were alone, and hope had fled;
We loved our country and our dead,
And could not shame them, so we stayed
the course, and were not so much afraid.

Dear God, that nightmare road, and then
That sea — we got there — We were men,
My eyes were blind, my feet were torn,
My soul sang like a bird at dawn.

I knew that death was but a door
I knew what we were fighting for;
Peace for the kids, our brothers freed,
A kinder world, A cleaner breed.

I'm but the son my mother bore,
A simple man, and nothing more,
But — God of strength and gentleness,
Be pleased to make me nothing less.
Help me, O God, when death is near to mock
    the haggard face of fear,
    that when I fall — if fall I must;
My soul may triumph in the dust.

CHAPTER EIGHT

Old Soldiers Never Die

"What a way to spend your 45th birthday." Mused Corporal Eddie Foulkes, D.C.M. M.M. Croix de Guerre, as he regained consciousness in a French farmer's field. Minutes before, the war for a moment seemed forgotten as he watched the farmer milk a cow. The warm sun imparting its pleasantries made him feel it was good to be alive. Gentle ripples from a nearby stream with a picturesque bridge provided generosity to the artist mind; inspiration for the poet and a teasing invitation to stop awhile for the enjoyments of a picnic.

But that day Eddie Foulkes banished from mind such sentiments. At 7 a.m. he had moved into the area together with an officer and seven men with orders to hold the bridge until 4 p.m. then demolish it and continue their objective of reaching nearby Dunkirk. Map and compass were no longer necessary for direction purposes. Dunkirk was easily recognisable by the tell-tale sign of huge clouds of smoke overshadowing the town. Eddie hadn't a clue as to what awaited him there except a strange feeling of hope in his heart.

Slowly senses returned and he remembered the Stuka bomber rudely invading the quiet country scene. The bomb blast almost turning him into a spaceman in the unscheduled flight. Depositing him many yards from his former position. His head screamed for intelligence in an effort to co-ordinate his faculties and stand up. For seconds that seemed a lifetime he stood affright. His uniform was bloodied and encased with flesh. Eddie wondered: 'whose?' Like a refreshing dawn mental awareness brought realisation — the blood was not his own and he was perfectly whole. The pit of his stomach turned over as he tried to tidy himself up by removing yards of cows flesh and inners draped about him. As for the farmer, he had completely disappeared off the face of the earth. "What about the others?" Sad memorials bespattered the herbage as the young Lieutenant and seven men lay dead. Furthermore, there was no bridge to guard. "Had I better go?" he asked himself.

Major Brandt's orders were to stay until 4 p.m. and that for Eddie decided the matter. Being an old soldier he believed: "A good soldier does what he is told, goes where he is sent and stays

where he is put." Few have heard of Eddie Foulkes but he epitom-
ises the discipline and spirit of the British Soldier. A quality rare
in the field of military history. One that causes the story of Dunkirk to be retold with pride.

Whilst standing his lonely guard, awaiting 4 p.m. to arrive,
Eddie looked at the remains of his dead comrades asking, "Why
them and not me?" Not a new question but one he has asked many
times. Memories stirred up that tragic Easter Sunday of 1916 in the
Cleethorpes Baptist Sunday School Hall. The hall housed soldiers
of the 3rd Battalion, The Manchester Regiment and at 20 years of
age Eddie knew the terror of war. Twice he left Cleethorpes for
France — twice he returned wounded in combat. The bombs from
Zeppelin LZ — 22 killed 38 soldiers and wounded 59. Amongst
them were friends, two being neighbours from Manchester and
another two men who joined the army together exactly 22 years
before. They soldiered together, and in their dying were not separ-
ated. Originally, they enlisted for a term of 21 years service, but
Lord Kitchener decreed that because of the war, all time expired
men should serve for an extra year. It was called the King's year.

On their last day of this extra period of service they arrived at Battalion H.G. to collect their discharge papers. The Regimental
Quartermaster Sergeant completed one man's documents, but the
second man's papers were incomplete. He was told the matter
would be rectified next day. The men resolved having joined
together so they would leave and the discharged man received permission to stay the night with his friend. Upon that fatal night
when death and injury visited the Sunday School Hall, more used
to the familiar sound of children's voices singing, 'What a Friend
we have in Jesus', Eddie Foulkes, resting in his bed, took a trip
through space as the blast from the bombs caused death and devestation. When he recovered amazement mingled with relief at the
realisation he had not sustained any injury.

Two nights later he was on guard duty none the worse for the
ordeal. Inwardly, grief for his friends held sway, now buried in a
communal grave in Cleethorpes Cemetary. Eddie never forgot
them. For 34 continuous years, each Easter Sunday, travelling
from Manchester to Cleethorpes he paid his homage.

Standing guard, a man has time for reflection, "Why them and
not me?" No audible voice responded in the quest to gain satisfy-
ing relief. Gazing upward into the night sky, so clear; then across
the calm waters of the Humber to Spurn Point, he longed for the
serenity within now displayed by nature. Eddie found himself
praying. Facing the sea he knelt and "made a compact with Deity,
that should I survive the war I would enter the ministry." Suddenly, the peace he sought entered as he felt the presence of God.

At 17 years of age, everything looked so promising for young
Eddie. The Methodist Church placed him on 'Full Plan' as a lay-

preacher. No mean achievement as a teenager. During his stay in Cleethorpes he enjoyed the fellowship at Mill Road Methodist Church. Preaching was upon his heart and each Sunday the preachers mannerisms and delivery held special attention. Local businessman Sir Thomas Robinson treated him like a son promising help should be desire to enter a theological college.

It was as if a sign had been given from God. He arose from his knees; feeling refreshed. Hope kindled with a determination to survive the war. Soon he would return to France to face two long years of war. Years of slaughter and carnage playing havoc with the young soldier's untested emotions.

Suffering from unhealed wounds, Eddie became a B1 medical category man and in March, 1918 helped to re-build the 59th Division wiped out in the Luddendorf offensive. The new recruits comprised of others in the B1 group but most had not seen active service. Drafted to the 36th Northumberland Fusiliers, on September 3rd, 1918 he was back in front line action. Now a corporal, well seasoned with veteran status at the ripe old age of 23 years.

The unit whose place they relieved at the front-line requested special surveillance for a two man patrol which failed to return following a mission to investigate a German machine-gun nest about a 100 yards away. Soon the ranks of the 36th Northumberland Fusiliers became thinned down as the gun spat death. Eddie asked Captain Wright for permission to deal with the gun. By now he had become used to some German trying to take his life away. Crawling along a dry ditch on the flank of the gun's position, cautiously he raised his head for a bearing. He found himself staring into the lifeless face of the soldier, who the day before accompanied his officer on patrol.

There was a neat bullet hole in the centre of his forehead, as though it had been drilled. Next a voice resounded, 'Bring me the Orders of the Day.' Nearby lay, in delerium, the missing officer. Eddie moved the wounded officer into the ditch, carrying him back to the company lines. Determined to complete the task, off he set for the second time. All seemed unusually quiet making him all the more conscious that one sound would reveal his mission. At last he sighted the evil gun with its crew of three. Crawling into the cover of a patch of uncut corn to the rear of the gun, Eddie schemed the plan of destruction. From a distance of twenty yards he threw a grenade, then ran and jumped into the strongpoint. Before the Germans could turn the gun in his direction, Corporal Eddie Foulkes showed them cold steel. Two of the crew died as the gibbet entered their stomachs; the third man ran away but Eddie let him go.

The nearby farm seemed a safe enough refuge for needed rest, giving time for frayed nerves to mend. Out of the haversack came the much worn and read copy of Kipling's verse. "The sons of

Mary seldom bother for they have inherited that good part." Abruptly, the reading ceased. Voices in song drew near. They weren't singing in English either. Peering through a crack in the farm buildings, the gallant soldier's heart almost stopped — more Germans pulling a cart on which lay several machine guns. 'Could they hear the beat of my heart?' he thought. Relief flooded his whole frame as he watched them move away. "Just collecting their dead, Thank God!'

Within twenty-four hours of returning to his company with valuable information concerning the enemies retreat to Aubers Ridge, Corporal Eddie was back in daring action. Sent out as a scout with the intent of bringing the Fusiliers into contact with the retreating Germans, Eddie stumbled upon a well laid trap. Undulating ground provided temporary cover as he debated the course of action necessary. Anticipating the point of attack, the Germans scientifically arranged their machine guns for a dose of instant death. Soon the company of Fusiliers would appear on the skyline to be 'hosed-down' by concentrated machine-gun fire. Quick deliberations caused mental gymnastics in Eddie's heated mind. In the next few minutes he would prove if he was a contender for the Olympic Games sprint or the now familiar letter to his next of kin commencing, 'We regret to inform you. . . .' Taking a deep breath he rose to his feet for the eventful 100 yards sprint. Machine gun bullets whined around his ears, spurts of soil appeared about his feet as the Germans relished a bit of target pratise. Fortunately for the budding athelete he ran the race for life in time stopping the Company reaching the summit of the slope.

Many of the 36th Northumberland Fusiliers, nicknamed 'John Bull's Boys' had never been in action before. In those days if you weren't dead sure what you were doing — you were sure dead. Corporal Eddie Foulkes and his counterparts endued the British Army with a quality rare and priceless. Eddie's Company Commander felt blessed with such a man around, entrusting him to come up with an idea designed to be one step ahead of German Intelligence by undertaking a cheeky operation under the cover of darkness. Before September 6th dawned, Eddie not only came up with the right idea but played the key role in moving, unknown to the enemy, 250 men during the night.

History in another sense was made that day, when Corporal Eddie Foulkes became the first medical category B1 man to be decorated. The high honour of the Military Medal the reward.

Six weeks later, Eddie's Company Commander felt his heroic corporal needed a rest. So when he sent out two platoons to probe a ridge at Wez Marquarte to verify a prisoner's statement that the place was not occupied, he decided it would be kind of Eddie for him to miss this simple recee. However, Eddie did not share his view and without arms or equipment thought he would spend his

Investiture of Eddie Foulkes

day off by joining a platoon under the command of Second Lieutenant Johnson. Arriving at their trench he found they had gone over the top. The sight of an officer's uneaten breakfast made him feel it really was a day off as he tucked-in. As soon as Mr. Johnson caught sight of the new arrival he dug into his vocabulary and resurrected some strong adjectives as an expression of his disgust. "Get back!" he ordered. But interrupted by a sound of firing from the farthest flank, Mr. Johnson changed the order to "Get over there, rally those men and silence that machine gun." Replied Eddie, "That's a tall order sir." The officer grinned: "You've asked for it, and I believe you can do it." Upon reaching the platoon, its leader dead, Eddie faced men receiving their introduction to combat. They looked scared as they followed their new leader into the enemy trench and watched him toss two Mills grenades. With haste they removed the dead German garrison, coming to life as they responded to Eddie's every instruction. Situated along the trench's traverse, Eddie occupied the central position. Amazement countenanced the mens' faces. Who was this strange corporal? For a moment with bewilderment they watched him plant a small Union Jack nailed to a stick. It reminded them of their childhood, a thing they did after building a sand-castle on the beach.

Cerimoniously placing the flag on the top, its donor viewed it not as a mascot or good-luck charm but christened it, 'my personal standard'. Here before his eyes, blowing in a gentle breeze an emblem of inspiration unfurled itself. Eddie experienced his spirit revive. Often on parades he would tremble at the reading of death sentences pronounced on cowards. It is human to shrink from death and pain; to run away. This Eddie determined would not be his lot.

From the trench, the ramparts of the French town of Lille could be seen. German trucks left the town full of soldiers with the express purpose of manning counter attacks. The men in the trench held out, they looked at the fluttering flag ministering courage after each raid.

A messenger arrived with orders to regroup under the command of Second Lieutenant Johnson. A roll call taken brought concern to Eddie. Three men he posted in exposed positions didn't know of the order to regroup because the messenger failed to inform them. One lived near Eddie in Manchester, Mr. Johnson didn't have time to give permission as Eddie went to look for them. An officer and three Germans setting up a machine gun were caught off guard as the one man rescue mission hurled a grenade. Reaching the target he found his friend fit and well. Returning down the lines a faint voice cried out, "Corporal, for my mother's sake don't leave me." Eddie turned to find a corporal of the West Ridings lying with a shattered leg. "Because I have a mother, I'll come back for you", he replied. Mr. Johnson agreed to delay their departure as Eddie kept his promise to the wounded corporal.

Second Lieutenant Johnson surveyed the situation. It was grim. The Germans appeared to hold the upper-hand and to make matters worse, fourteen of his men lay wounded. Somehow he must get them back to the Company lines. It was a job. Eddie led the procession with a limping man's arm around his shoulder. Whilst testing a tree log forming a bridge across a barbed wire-filled stream, a burst of machine gun fire hit the limping man in the face. The gun 150 yards away pinned down the party. Every movement of the wounded brought on a burst of fire and each hit caused some poor lad to scream. Eddie found himself laying flat on his back with his head pressed against the trunk of a tree. He did so want to hide from those jets of iron death. He shouted: "Listen, lads, think you are in chapel. Let us now sing 'Jesus lover of my soul'". For a time the Germans remained silent as Eddie led his congregation. The lads joined in doing justice to the lovely Wesley hymn.

With heart and hope they sang: "Other refuge have we none, Hangs our helpless souls on Thee, Leave, Oh, leave us not alone, Still support and comfort us." Some were too weak to sing. Others weren't sure of all the words so Eddie at times became the lead singer. When he came to the part, "Cover our defenceless heads, With the shadow of Thy wing", the West Riding corporal nursing his shattered leg called, "He will, corporal, He will." By now the life-blood of the West Riding corporal had almost drained away. He knew death stared at him. The padre gave comfort asking if there was a last wish — "Yes! Read me the 14th chapter of John's gospel, and tell my mother that my heart is not troubled, I shall soon be in my Father's house of many mansions." David's family did not suspect he knew his Bible so well and the padre's letter telling them of his last wish helped them to bear their great sorrow. "Keep singing corporal." Commanded one of the wounded as others seconded the motion. Eddie sang until he was hoarse. Like a devil's chorus, the Germans punctuated the Chapel meeting with burst upon burst of machine-gun fire.

Help was on the way and realising this the Germans brought up reinforcements. Now quite close enemy voices became clear: "Shoot pig Englander, shoot." Over came their potato-masher bombs. The men could hear the thrower call: "Tea up, Tommy, Tea up, Tommy", in mockery of the British who used to shout when they threw a grenade, "Stir your tea up with that, Gerry." Three men, new to action went into an enemy trench to surrender. An officer approached to receive them, but Second Lieutenant Johnson snatched a rifle, jumped out of his ditch, ran across into the German trench and drove the three frightened men back to their places. To make his journey worthwhile he shot the German Officer. With booming voice he shouted: "I'll shoot any officer or man, who talks about surrender."

As Eddie's 'Chapel congregation', made their escape, Germans came down their trench. Others across open ground, firing from the hip. Mr. Johnson stood his ground, emptying his revolver into the enemy. Nearby lay a wounded man whom Mr. Johnson raised and cradled in his arms. Meanwhile, Eddie used the dead West Riding corporal as cover, keeping the enemy busy until Mr. Johnson could join him. Through a torrent of fire they reached a safe trench now manned by reinforcements. The only surviving officer of the West Ridings, Lieutenant Smith embraced Eddie: "I thought you were dead. Lend me your pay book I'm recommending you for the Victoria Cross."

Of the 160 men of the 36th Northumberland Fusiliers and West Riding Regiment who began the assault, only 70 returned. Eddie's Fusiliers during the action received 1 Victoria Cross; 1 Distinguished Service Order; 8 Military Medals; 2 Distinguished Conduct Medals and 2 Military Crosses. To add to his Military Medal, Eddie gained the award of the Distinguished Conduct Medal. For weeks he wondered if rumour of an award of the Victoria Cross was true. A recommendation had been made but it was not until Christmas Eve, 1918 that he knew. Major General Sir Neville Symthe, V.C. sent for him. In his hand an Army Council telegram. "You are the proper one to take this to Mr. Johnson." As the general's orderly, Eddie requested permission to write an account of Mr. Johnson's conduct. Finding the English language totally inadequate to describe the heroic officer's valour, words mingled with emotions in completing the task. "We fought together, compact, unanimous, and I felt the pride of leadership."

A company messenger arrived on the scene bearing a note: "Brigadier Stansfield desires Lieut. Johnson, V.C. to dinner this evening." The messenger received a ten franc note with a command: "Tell the sender you can't find me. This corporal's name should be placed with mine — I'm taking him to be photographed."

London Gazette: 26th December 1918

CITATION
Second Lieutenant James Johnson, 36th Battalion Northumberland Fusiliers. For most conspicuous bravery and devotion to duty on October, 14th 1918, during operations by strong patrols. He repelled frequent counter attacks, and for six hours under heavy fire he held back the enemy. When at length he was ordered to retire he was the last man to leave the advanced position, carrying a wounded man. Three times subsequently this officer returned and brought in badly wounded men under intense machine gun fire. His valour, cheerfulness and utter disregard of danger inspired all."

Debris and death strewn across the pleasant country scene puzzled the old soldier. "Why?" he asked himself. Bringing to remembrance bold statements about the Great War. The war in which he gave his all. The war in which Haig commanded in one day more men than Marlborough and Wellington in the whole of their careers. Some said: "It was the war to end all wars."

Anger gripped Eddie as faces from the past paraded before him. When a word is a word of experience then the experience of him who uses it will define its meaning.

Paschendale ... fighting kneedeep in liquid mud, where good men fell but no sign marks their grave. Sergeant Leroy ... I have a trobbing head, sometimes as I lie in my bed. Thinking of my pal in the wire athirst with his belly on fire. He who had been filled with laughter, moaning, "Please God, I want water." That German ...

> I choked, my grip on his throat,
> My teeth in his jowl which silenced his howl,
> We met in a trench and wrestled at length
> I called 'Kamerade', but he hit me hard
> We fought to survive, one remained alive
> The harvest I reaped was absence of sleep,
> And feelings of fright that came in the night.

The heavens seemed as brass as he pondered: "Was it all in vain?" Seeking the benefit of a refreshing dawn from the exhaustion of shaking the emotional tree coupled with the frustration of unanswered questions; the lonely soldier shuffled his feet. The movement disturbed an ant hill. Watching the creatures engaged in their work he raised his boot. "You are at the mercy of my whim, I can end your existence." Lines from Shakespeare were recalled: "as flies to wanton boys so are we to gods. They kill us for their sport." Like a flash of lightning a mediatorial voice gatecrashed the executioner's thoughts: "If you spare them, God will spare you." Eddie fell to his knees in prayer, pouring out his soul to God. A more composed man arose: somehow he would survive this war as well and when he got home would place a "Thank You God" advertisement in the Manchester Evening News.

Major Brandt's order to stay put until 4 p.m. received an unexpected challenge. Thinking: "3.30 p.m. not much longer to go", Eddie's resolve to stay a further thirty minutes quickly changed. The rumble of enemy tanks nearby, heading in his direction dictated a new motto "discretion is the better part of valour." After firing a token shot, quickly he clambered across the debris of the bridge, thanking God he was fit enough in contemplating reaching Dunkirk. Along the main road a British Army lorry stopped to pick up the lonely passenger. Eddie never thought to ask where they were headed: it seemed such a wasted question. Wearily, dishevelled comrades made a place for their new companion. Too

88

tired to talk but each sharing a common hope of escape from the clutches of their oppressor.

"At last! I'm safe!" Seemed to be written upon each face and Eddie very much wanted to be part of the picture. The words were fitting for a lullaby as sleep seemed to be the order of the day. Suddenly, a sheet of hot air, a rude intruder by now quite familiar, lifted Eddie out of the lorry. Sitting on the grass verge dazed and wondering if he was in heaven, reality returned by the sensation of his scorched body screaming with pain. Momentarily paralysed through fear this gave way to his whole frame shaking as if subjected to a constant electrical current. More effective than any sergeant major's voice, orders yelled down the corridors of his soul: "Get a grip man!" In his heat obsessed brain fighting for saneness, this much blown-about man unconsciously checked himself over reporting: "Thank God! Nothing missing". The lorry lay in a mess, hit by a bomb or shell, the passengers lay dead. His uniform in ribbons, Eddie staggered down the road in a state of shock repeating the oft asked question: "Why them and not me?"

Senses regained, the sad figure put his nose in the direction of Dunkirk. Each step became a step of determination as he began to feel more like his old self. Jokes about Manchester and its rain will never cease but to Corporal Eddie Foulkes in that moment of time it loomed as the most beautiful place on earth. The small things of life, often overlooked in their complacent acceptance danced in colours unseen before, as lessons not learned in the light found a willing pupil during the darkness of this episode. Benefits were turned into blessings as he assessed and revalued his whole life's lot. "Wonder what the wife is doing?" he deliberated. Actually, she was looking upon herself as a possible widow. The 716 Construction Company, Royal Engineers, recruited by Manchester Corporation comprising of 250 men from their Surveyors, Engineers and Architects Departments, sent to France in late 1939 in order to undertake a project of preparing concrete runways for airfields, now reformed in Suffolk. Eddie was posted missing.

The welcome sight of khaki and someone to talk to brought sunshine into a miserable day. The man looked wonderfully turned out in full webbing packs. He told Eddie of his life of crime in pre-war days but the opportunities of the last few days were too wonderful to describe. During a rest period, opening the packs, he produced his wares. Silver Chalices from Churches and a vast array of gold and silver taken from various French jewellery shops. Eddie resolved the quicker he got away from his criminal companion, the safer he would feel.

Now hungry, the solitary French farmhouse extended its own tantalising invitation. Inside were a mother and baby. The baby, fed on beer was the fattest he had ever seen. Willingly, the woman sat him down at the table, serving up a meal which more than satisfied Eddie's need. The woman busied herself in preparing for further guests. Ashen faced, with hands raised high, Eddie stood at the table. The new guests had arrived. In perfect English, the German officer politely told Eddie to sit down. The war hardly existed as conversation at the table bore the informality of old friends sharing an evening together. Personal talk ensued and the officer appeared pleased at the mention of Manchester, remarking that his father used to work at the Midland Hotel. The meal over, with apology the officer excused himself from the table, stating he and his men must go. In the meantime, Eddie would be held in the barn until they returned.

A large padlock graced the barn door; outside a one man sentry. Peering through a crack in the wooden wall, Eddie watched the sentry get comfortable, seated on an upturned wheelbarrow. The thoughts of a prisoner-of-war camp orchestrated horrific notes. Searching the barn, he found a spade and started to dig beneath the rear end wall, providing a tunnel of escape. Creeping round to the front of the barn, the sentry, still seated on the wheelbarrow had really made himself comfortable, removing his steel helmet and now wearing a forage cap. With one blow, the excapee brought the spade down upon the guard's head. Sufficient to give the man a few hours sleep. Eddie hoped he didn't brain the poor man. It was far easier to kill an enemy at a distance, but to share a meal then kill him presented a different proposition.

Back en-route for Dunkirk, later a British Army lorry picked him up. At first, memories of the previous lift caused hesitations. However near exhaustion he permitted helping hands to hoist him into the vehicle. The appearance of the men inside matched the last human cargo he had travelled with, except for one man. He had seen that look in the eye and foaming mouth, countless times. The tell-tale sign of a man out of control. Suddenly, the strange one jumped up, foam oozing from his mouth. Laughing: releasing the safety catch on his rifle, he started shooting up the wagon. Everyone froze. Terrified! Seeing a large spanner on the floor, Eddie grasped it. Scuffling with the man he brought the spanner hard down upon his bare head. The lifeless body falling over the rail-board of the vehicle. "What next?" he wondered.

The roads into Dunkirk were now crammed with men. They came from every direction, British, Belgian and French. In the darkness the cloud of smoke overshadowing the towns turned into a glaring fire shooting high into the sky. From the sea, the navy shelled the Germans, lighting up the night sky with a white glow. Driving through Dunkirk, Eddie took in the scenery. Hardly a building appeared to be left standing; wrecked vehicles littered the streets. Bodies lay where they had fallen as through the fire and smoke the living wended their way to the beach. He read the look on passing faces translating a determination inwardly he shared.

Eddie thought of the many sermons he'd sat under on the frightening subject of "The Fires of Hell". None reached him more forcibly than his present nightmare environment, as once more the earth tremored with the thunder of a nearby explosion. "So this is the gateway to freedom", he mused, as he felt in his pocket for something to chew and calm his frayed nerves. Alas! the cupboard was bare. Something quite new for since joining the army as a teenager, habitually he carried a hard boiled egg; a bar of chocolate and a packet of 'Peak Frean's' biscuits. The events of the past few days shut out any opportunity to replenish stocks.

From La Panne beach aboard the former Isle of Wight paddle-steamer *Gracie Fields* now a Royal Navy minesweeper and bound for Dover, Eddie could have sung 'Sally, Sally' with gusto. About 750 men aboard looked back at the beach sighing relief and gratitude to the navy.

Up above the German Stuka pilot must have wondered if this was the English Channel or the Mississippi as he spotted the paddle-boat. Not being a 'Gracie Fields' fan, with lethal accuracy he came in low and machine-gunned the crowded decks. The first bomb dropped down the steamer's funnel and the explosion from the second bomb which fell amongst the crowded troops sucked all the air from Eddie's body, flinging it into the sea.

The explosion in the boiler room shattered steam pipes and killed everyone in both engine and boiler rooms. Those who were not killed by the explosion died horribly from the scalding steam.

The upperdeck, shrouded in clouds of steam, which settled like a thick mist, hid the shambles of twisted steel, decapitated bodies and human flesh strewn about the rigging and rails.

With rudder jammed at an angle and no one alive to stop engines, the *Gracie Fields* went round in circles at full speed. Brilliant seamanship enabled two schuyts to make fast alongside and take off as many men they could carry. The minesweeper *Pangbourne* giving rescue to a further eighty. By now the *Gracie Fields* boilers had lost most of their steam as the *Pangbourne* took her in tow and started again for England. Some hours later the *Gracie Fields* began to sink, so the *Pangbourne* slipped the tow and took off her crew.

On board the destroyer *Scimitar* a sailor handed Eddie a mug of tea. His fingers were so numb he could hardly hold it. The hot liquid scalding his mouth as he spat it on the deck, his mouth filled with a bitter taste from the salt water he'd swallowed. The sailor bent over: "Drink your own good health chum", Eddie's eyes were stinging as he looked up trying to make out the form of his kind benefactor. "Me and my mate thought you were dead so we were going to chuck you overboard to make room for someone else, when that Welsh Guards major over there, him with the red moustache saw you move", Eddie nodded, painfully turning his head in the direction of the Major, yet not focussing properly. The sailor continued: "we stripped you of your clobber and boots, dipped two blankets in hot water and wrapped you in them until you came round."

The destroyer's bofors guns disturbed the conversation, spitting angry projectiles at a German Stuka overhead. Eddie found his voice: "If that plane up there hits this ship then I don't want to know about it." The spirit that had brought him so far now stanced in a couldn't care less attitude. Wrapping one blanket around himself for a kilt, the other for a coat, he went through the motions of being alive heading for the nearby iron ladder which took him below decks. He was not alone. Dozens of troops engaged in drying out their clothes on the ship's huge hot plate. Shocked! Exhausted! Dis-spirited! Eddie sat down with head in hands and cried.

It had been a long time since the sound of people cheering was heard. The noise up above resounded of jubilation. It extended an invitation of its own. Back on deck he saw the crew of the Goodwin Lightship cheering and the soldiers on deck were cheering back. However, not all joined in the happy chorus. Amidst the excitement a young soldier lay on the deck all alone. Around his throat a blood stained bandage. Kneeling down, Eddie lifted the lad's head and cradled it in his arm, saying, "Can I do anything for you?" The lad croaked: "I want a priest". He started to mumble: "I saw Jesus on the sands. I talked with Jesus on the sands." His words became fainter as energy expired. "Would you like me to pray for you?" Eddie whispered in his ear, receiving an immediate acknowledging nod. The men were still cheering when Eddie prayed: "Father into Thy hands I commend his spirit". Blood seeped through the bandage, not another word was spoken as gently his head fell forward.

Eddie Foulkes did not recover health until September, 1943. According to what folk refer to as "the law of averages", it is amazing he survived at all. Today, at 82 years of age, keen in mind he still asks; "Why them, and not me?"

Perhaps in this moment of time I could venture to deal with your tormenting question, furnishing an answer which upon reflection, I trust and pray will bring blessing and illumination in these evening years of your life.

Dear Eddie,

You ask: "Why them, and not me?" It's not an easy question to grapple with, nor one which I hope to supply a complete answer to. Nevertheless, I'm sure some of the following remarks will help you in receiving a revelation hitherto unknown. Even when I have done, do not forget that human history, with all its sufferings is now and has at all times been, subject to the overriding Will of

Eddie Foulkes, D.C.M., M.M., C. de G., 82 years old

Divine Providence.

Our reasoning faculty is a gift from God and it is our obligation both to cultivate it and use it. Yet there are limits for our confidence in our reason exceeds its competence. Perhaps you feel the army robbed you of the life you set your heart upon. It must be kept in mind also that God's leadings are always intrinsically reasonable, whether the reasonableness is apparent at the moment or not. The unfolding of events will vindicate us, rather than expose our folly.

It would not be far fetched to state it is a 'miracle' you are alive at all. As a young man you underwent terrors unknown to the youth of today. You soldiered with the British Army, which even now is the most efficient in the world. Your discipline lives today. As a Dunkirk Veteran you declare it was not a defeat but a victory — a victory of the human spirit. The situation in Northern Ireland conveys sad news but your discipline and spirit pervades the British Army there. Under great provocation, the lessons of modern history should make all thankful it is the British Army under provocation and none other.

When people are out to 'knock' authority as something evil and tilt established ways, your voice is needed! Thank God for the quality of leadership you experienced, how we sore need it now. As long as you've breath in your body, speak of the efficacy of prayer. Obviously, the influence of godly men like Sir Thomas Robinson of Cleethorpes rubbed off on you. Continue to speak of great men who like him found the humility to spend hours in agonising prayer until the overdue fishing trawler returned safely. How we now need men who will pray as anarchy sows its ugly seeds in the nation.

The passing of your two sons within a space of 24 hours sent your world crashing. You and your good wife shared a grief few could enter into. Very easily bitterness could have ruled your hearts, yet how beautifully you wrote:—

A touch at my elbow
I look around,
Drop the daisies — marguerites
They lightly fell upon the wood
That closed for aye the little form
of Derek, — brief visitant
To this sad world
One of the flowers fell over the side
And rested its due upon the casque
of the elder, Roy — who had breathed
seven times the life of the babe below.
The mourners took a lingering gaze
And slowly wended down the path

94

Which led to the noise, the worldly din,
With hat in hand
We strolled away,
A glimpse of heaven fresh in our minds:
The whisper of angels in our ears.
The mother smiled.
The father talked.
The least affected wept
And left behind
The sad Benign
Chief mourner — Christ
Who had said
"Tis not the will
Of the Father in heaven
That these little ones should perish."

God comes to us in the darkness and takes the hurts of our lives and binds them up. Little did you think the Baptist Church where the funeral service took place would be the venue for your own resurrection as afterwards you found a place in the work programme of that Church.

The providential leadings of God will never be to our ordering but through the tears and heartache you found the Grace of God adequate for every need.

The torment of mind brought on by "the murderous things I'd done", architected a fixed barrier between yourself and Christian Service, certainly any form of pulpit ministry. Yet the mercy of God is greater than tongue or pen can ever tell. Remember when you wrote:—

I used to walk the street at night,
oppressed by some remembered sight.
Saw dead friends ghosts everywhere,
Jumped a shell hole that was not there.
Heard the 'shoot pig Englander' shout,
when there was no shouter about.
For long I tried to keep hidden
my neurasthenic condition
There was not then psychiatry
to give relief to such as me.
In my despair I turned to prayer.
God's Spirit told me not to care
I found in Christ the anodyne
which brought peace to my troubled mind
Whatever else has vanished away
What I was given came to stay.

Eddie! Your message is needed.
Tell it to the downhearted and downtrodden. To the oppressed;

Eddie Foulkes — leading remembrance parade, Manchester, 1974

to those who have lost their way, sinking into the great abyss of despair. Tormented night and day by a conscience ill at ease.

You have declared the words of Jesus as being relevant for today, when he said: "love your neighbour as yourself". Within God-given bounds, self-love is the key to real living. A day dawned, when in your helplessness you cast yourself upon the mercy of God. Begging help for your disordered life. The miracle of a 'new birth' created a self-respect, hitherto unknown, releasing determination for self-preservation and protection. Desiring the highest welfare for your own soul. Selfishness took wings with the understanding that love is not love until it is given away. In turn you began to give out a God-given respect for your neighbour anxious for their well being.

Locked up in the secret chambers of God is the answer to: "Why them, and not me?" Push the tantalising question into the arena of acceptance and Praise God! Thank Him for the privilege of living an eventful life and the accomplishments that have ensued.

Surely, the ten years spent as pastor of an Independent Chapel not only gave to you the desire of your heart but even now bears fruit of eternal value.

Today the Dunkirk Veterans Association boasts over 80 branches. In 1945 the honour befell you to bring it to birth with the formation of the 'Dunkirk Survivor's Association', which in 1953 gave way to the 'Dunkirk Veteran's Association', of which again you were a founder member.

Well, my friend, I must close as I want to get on with the remainder of the book. Before I do, may I remind you of some words from your sermon at the 1966 Rememberance Service:—

.... It must follow that God is asking us, "Have you engaged yourself in the task I spared you for?" As though we were artists and He said, "I gave you colours, where is your picture?" Or, "I gave you music; where is your song?" Or, "I gave you breath, where is your living soul?" I do believe you and I will be judged by our response to this question. . . . As someone said to Sir Douglas Haig during the war's darkest day: "I hope, Sir, that you are not too discouraged?" To which Haig relied: "A Christian man cannot be discouraged in the same world as God."

Keep preaching that message!
Every Blessing!
Your friend,
  Fred Grossmith

Truly 'Old Soldiers Never Die' — They Only Fade Away! Will the spirit of the Eddie Foulkes of this world ever fade away? I pray not.

An ardent Royalist, often his newspaper writings are attacked by those who only have disintegration of the nation in mind with frightening alternatives to offer. Eddie believes: "A monarch is the symbol of the peoples' unity and deserves the devotion of her subjects."

On one occasion he was called upon to escort Her Majesty the Queen Mother when she inspected a gathering of V.C. and D.C.M. holders on Horse Guards Parade. When introduced to Her Majesty he was moved to say: "Now I have met you Ma'am, I understand why his late Majesty the King fell in love with you." At the end of the parade he was given a spray from the royal bouquet. Sir Winston Churchill felt otherwise and gave him a ticking-off.

The Manchester Branch of the Dunkirk Veterans Association of which he is founder, life-member and Chairman exceeds a membership of 500 veterans; the largest in Britain. Eddie Foulkes is proud to be a Dunkirk man. Such pride permeating his composition:—

SONG OF THE D.V.A.

We were a phalanx elite,
Who by a fighting retreat
Evading threatened defeat
Dented the Panzers' conceit.
There could be no other word
A miracle had occurred.
We were ordinary men
But the crisis time came when
The necessity arose,
To meet the onslaught of foes
When they essayed their sortie
On May tenth, nineteen-forty.
The spirit of Corunna
Was evident that summer
What Munich killed had rebirth,
Britain's spirit walked the earth
The liberties of mankind
To us by God were assigned,
We proved equal to the task
And did far more than was asked.

The La Panne and Dunkirk sands,
Where we made our gallant stand,
Symbolise the memory
of those nine days' history.
The Pilgrimage, grief's vesture,
Is our annual gesture,
Of respect to those who died,

Whose blood that beach sanctified.
Not for them the ecstasy
of the final victory
From our sight they may be gone
But they with us are as one.

CHAPTER NINE

1940
DUNKIRK VETERANS ASSOCIATION
or
THE PEOPLE WITHOUT A MEDAL

Patron: The Mayor of Dunkirk
Vice Patrons: The Mayor of Dover
  The Mayor of Folkestone
  The Mayor of Margate
  The Mayor of Ramsgate
President: General Sir Peter Hunt, G.C.B., D.S.O., O.B.E., F.B.I.M.
Vice Presidents: Prigadier J.B. Gawthorpe, C.B.E., T.D.
  Group Capt. L. Cheshire, V.C., D.S.O., D.F.C.
  Lt. Col. A.B. Brown, T.D.
  Lt. Col. R.H. Camrass, M.B.E., T.D., LL.B.
  Lt. Col. C.P. Rigby, T.D.
  The Rt. Hon. Lord Carew, C.B.E.
  Major General D.A.L. Wade, C.B., O.B.E., M.C.
  Brigadier the Rt. Hon. Sir John Smyth, Bt. V.C., M.C.
Chairman: Major General V.H.J. Carpenter, C.B., M.B.E.
Vice Chairman: Capt. L.A. Jackson
Hon. General Secretary: H. Robinson, Esq., M.B.E.
Hon. Chaplain: Rev. L. Aitken, M.B.E.
Hon. General Treasurer: W.C. Brown Esq.
Hon. General Welfare Officer G. Benton, Esq.

The Association was founded in Leeds on the 24th November, 1953 by eleven veterans of the British Expeditionary Force (France 1940).

Gradually news of the Association spread and branches were formed in Doncaster, Bradford, Manchester, London and Bury. Today, there are over eighty branches in the United Kingdom, six in Australia, three in New Zealand, one in Canada, one in N. America and one in Rhodesia.

Within the Association I have discovered a very wonderful atmosphere of *esprit de corps*. Something rarely found in this modern world. I pray they may nurture this proud 'possession' as their

100

monthly gatherings take place, bound to each other through an experience that will remain until their last breath. Who can forget a miracle? Who can forget the day when a chapter of history was written in the blood of their generation?

The beginnings of the Dunkirk Veterans Association found birth in the heart of non other than Eddie Foulkes, D.C.M., M.M., C de G. In April 1945 as chairman and founder he launched the 'Dunkirk Survivors Association'. Although giving way in 1953 to the present Association, the original Aims and Objects remain unchanged:—

a) To utilise in civil life the fine spirit of the 'Beaches'.
b) To honour the 'Fallen' and to sponsor the interests of their dependents.
c) To remind the community of its indebtedness to the men of the B.E.F.

The first Sunday in June would be appointed as 'Dunkirk Memorial Sunday' and the idea of an annual Pilgrimage was written into the Manifesto. As the Association grew so did the conviction that they should be rewarded by a special Campaign Star, rejecting openly Prime Minister Clement Attlee's suggestion that the then recently instituted War Medal should satisfy them.

In 1976, Pauline Richards travelled with the Folkestone Branch on her first Pilgrimage and returned home a different person. What she saw and heard is contained in the following moving tribute:—

DUNKIRK — By Pauline Richards

I'd heard of the spirit of Dunkirk, of course I had, who not?
I went on a Dunkirk Pilgrimage expecting? who knows what?
I found a group of people who blended into one
When on parade, I saw them, though the fighting now was done.

Their chests ablaze with medals, in age heads still held high,
Some with limbs gone, just top wounds healed, and I asked,
Oh why, God, Why?
Did they have to suffer on that beach and have their youth so crushed?
Each one there, male and female, knowing them that death had brushed.

I could not join them on the beach, I felt I'd not the right
But I listened to their voices, singing in the sunshine bright,
I am prouder to be English than I've ever been before,
If it had not been for these heroic folk, who knows what was in store?

I went into the cemetery, a single cross I placed
On the grave of an unknown soldier, 19 years, dear God,
Dear God, what waste;
I looked at each and everyone and silently I prayed,
Thank you, bless you, everyone, to all who died and stayed,
To all the people who survived, again my silent prayer,
When you were needed, you stood and were counted,
Thank God that you were there.

Each year from all parts of the United Kingdom, the Commonwealth and the Americas, veterans set course for the rendezvous Place Jean Bart, Dunkirk. Usually around 10.45 a.m. on the Sunday morning thousands of veterans, under the watchful eye of Parade Organiser Veteran Harold Robinson, M.B.E., form ranks. Divided into companies, the Company Commanders are easily identifiable by their Official Armband. With Standards held high and medals proudly displayed — all await orders from the Parade Marshall.

With majesty, the impressive statue of Jean Bart occupies the central position. This buccaneer rose to Admiral of the Royal French Fleet and in one sense he too could be classified a veteran as the statue was about all that was left undamaged in 1940.

With bands playing, the townspeople gather to watch the parade proceed down Rue Clemenceau past the Belfry of Dunkirk, commonly called the Tower and built in the fifteenth century. Before the parade would have fully passed, the bells of the Tower chime their hourly bars of the Cantata to Jean Bart. Opposite stands Saint Eloi Church, built very shortly after the Belfry and housing the grave of Jean Bart.

Reaching the Town Hall, eyes cannot help but take in the equestrian statue of Louis XIV. But as the Veterans enter the Town Hall, a magnificent stained glass window picturing the return of Jean Bart after his victory at Texel is a fitting greeting to the returning 'warriors'.

Following an official reception at Dunkirk Town Hall, a ceremony of wreath laying is attended to with much solemnity at the Town Memorial.

In the afternoon, once again the beaches become 'A Church on the Dunes' when the Chaplain to the Association, the Rev. Leslie Aitken, M.B.E., conducts the Memorial Service. Memories are relived, emotions stirred, openly and unashamedly some shed tears. Just like the lepers in the Gospels, grateful men return to give God thanks for their deliverance. Dunkirk men have no illusions as to the source of their deliverance. The cover page of the official Printed Order of Service, sums it all up:

In Thanksgiving to Almighty God for the deliverance at His

Jean Bart Square, Dunkirk

Also

in commemoration of those who gave their lives during those eventful days in the cause of Freedom!

Wreaths are laid at the Allied Memorial, then from the beaches the veterans board coaches for the ten minute journey to Dunkirk Military Cemetery, carefully tended by the French as a Memorial to British dead. A sea of small white headstones bear testimony to the young men, "Whose Name Liveth For Evermore."

As the years roll by the ranks grow thinner; a fact attested by the growing obituary column contained in the attractive 'D.V.A. Journal'. Each Pilgrimage becoming a 'last visit' for groups of men resolved never to return again for while the spirit is willing the flesh grows weaker. But time cannot erase their memory of deliverance or snuff out the 'fire of thanksgiving' kindled upon the altar of their hearts.

For Veteran John Kelly, the 1975 Pilgrimage proved to be the most dramatic of all the following reprint from the Northampton Chronicle and Echo unfolds the story of his last return:

DEATH OF A PIPER

Every summer, members of the Dunkirk Veterans Association return to the scene of one of history's great moments. Numbered amongst the dwindling ranks are the men of the Northampton and Milton Keynes branch.

As the years go by our numbers are slowly eroded, the ranks grow thinner. Yet the strength that held the band togehter in the dark days of 1940 becomes even stronger as those ranks close around the few that are left, and each pilgrimage brings its own story of tragedy, its own pattern in life's kaleidoscope. In this year, when we recall those happenings of 35 years ago, we find no exception.

He led the contingent of Dunkirk Veterans proudly. His grey head was held as a soldier should, high and level, the back straight. The pipes that he held so lovingly gave the song that inspired a long swinging gait to those that followed in his wake. They too, as all followers of a piper, felt a pride in their being that only comes to men at times such as these.

The drum's beat and the skirl of the pipes brought on a new dimension to the scene. Suddenly, whilst his heart gave power to the pipe's song, came a stumble . . . just two faltered steps . . . and the grey head lay there amid the sand.

The sands from that beach he had known so well blew around those greying temples, and as he lay there a rattle came into his throat — a noise so many of us had heard long ago. We worked with feverish ugency — hoping all the time, yet not daring to hope. They came and took him away. Those grey hairs would be no more with song of the piper. He had died playing his own lament. . . .

The pipes had sung of those green hills of my highland home. I wonder if he found them. If so, it was here at Dunkirk, where so many of his comrades had found their own green hills. His brothers joined together to mourn his passing, and as those pipers "played him out" to the strains of "Amazing Grace", the humming of five thousand of his comrades gave their share to the last dirge.

The men who had travelled the globe, from Canada, from Australia, from all corners of the United Kingdom to honour their dead now stood with bowed heads, to do homage to him. The flotilla of "little ships", the Spitfire . . . the Hurricane . . . the Lancaster . . . all joined in our last tribute.

As they dipped their wings in a last salute, it was fitting he was here to receive it, amid the sands where he had marched long ago . . . leading his comrades so willingly to see those green hills far away.

For John Kelly, Piper, the last lament had been his greatest!

JOHN M.P. CURTIN

The Dunkirk Veterans Association is a family bound by strong cords. A little known side of their work is the constant activity of their Welfare Officers engaged in caring for the under privileged and rapidly growing list of comrades laid aside through sickness. All officers from the overworked and much travelled General Secretary, the never resting 'Journal' editor down to the local branch committee members give their services voluntarily: without financial reward. For them the 'Dunkirk Spirit' is not a mere part of historic terminology — rather a baptism they received with fruits that remain.

No one has written a complete 'Dunkirk Story' or ever will. For each veteran is — 'the story'. I have yet to find an Errol Flynn type who won the war on his own. True! Many received recognition in the award of gallantry medals but the mark of the Association is a common bond and designation — 'veterans'. Always mindful of the days when in their helplessness God made them the recipients of 'a miracle of deliverance'.

Veteran A. Howison of Leeds provides an insight to the personality of the Association by an analysis of the symbolism of The Standard of the D.V.A. The Standard is to the Association what the Regimental Colour is to the soldier. Both enshrine the tradition of service to God, the Queen and country.

Dunkirk Memorial, Dover, Kent

The Spearhead, pointing to heaven, signifies our duty to God.
The Crest in the centre is our Association badge, which reminds us of our fallen comrades.
The Blue reminds us of those who died on service, on land, sea or in the air.
The Red reminds us of those who passed through the ordeal of fire.
The two Tassels at the end of the cord represent the beginning and end of life.
The Cord itself represents the golden road along which all good veterans should pass during their lifetime here.
All these ideals are bound together by the Fringe which signifies the brotherhood and comradeship of the Association.

Nearly 40 years have gone by but still fresh stories come to light, daily new poems are written. In fact I have never come across so many poets. Often veterans wonder what it would have been like to have been the last soldier on the beaches. Only those who went into captivity know the answer. Undoubtedly, Veteran R. Eccles of Hull must lay claim to being one of the last to escape. A World War I veteran, twice mentioned in Dispatches, at Bray Dunes he nearly missed the boat, being dragged through the water by a naval Petty Officer as the destroyer H.M.S. *Anthony* put to sea, with the enemy racing down the beach.

Whenever people find fellowship together, someone in the group has the gift of humour, yet more often than not the humorous one also has a deadly serious and sombre side. Veteran Fred Kitchener of Northampton saw action in many theatres of war, faced sticky situations which made him wonder if his hour had come. He has the gift of humour encased in humility:

> I did one brave deed I will have you note
> It was in the heat of battle a Jerry had my Officer by the throat
> And as the Officer owed me ten bob — it really got my goat.
> I raised my rifle and gave that Jerry all I'd got
> And best of all got my ten bob back on the spot!

Of course Fred Kitchener is another of the D.V.A. poets. In serious moments he has often wondered, having lived through the terrors of Dunkirk, how he would have behaved if fate had called upon him to be the last soldier on Dunkirk beach.

JUNE 4th 1940
DUNKIRK: "OUR" Last Soldier

British Military Section of Dunkirk Cemetary

The Day was Hot and the lone Khaki clad figure was still wondering how he came to be all alone it must have been that last bomb dropped among them his mates must have thought he was dead, and left him. However, it was only concussion, he must have laid there for the best part of a day.

He moved stealthily on to the beach — rifle at the ready — there was an uncanny silence — his red tired eyes wearily scanned the beach here, there, everywhere were still silent figures — some lying gracefully as if reverently laid out, others were sprawled in grotesque positions, but one thing was certain — dead they all were.

He looked at the carnage the Stukas had wrought — they had done their job well. Dunkirk was burning and most parts just heaps of rubble. A destroyer lay off the beach broken in half.

Suddenly a lone Stuka roared over the beach and angrily the gaunt figure raised his rifle and fired desperately at the enemy plane — his first tracer bullet gave his whereabouts and the Stuka banked and came down at him, screaming like a thousand banshees from hell — guns blazing. He missed this diminutive figure, who was only 19 years old yesterday, because he had learned more in the last three weeks of constant combat than he would have learned from a year's study of Army manuals. He was in the shelter of an abandoned bren carrier in half a second flat. It was easy for him to forsee the Stukas' every move and take the necessary evasive action, firing his rifle all the time. The Stuka pilot, realising he was dealing with a canny enemy, gave a last long burst from his guns and disappeared over the horizon.

Thankfully the soldier looked around him and finally took up position facing the town from where he knew the enemy would come. He gave little thought to the fact that he would be facing the entire German army. He took a long cool drink from his water bottle and he thought how the hell had everyone been evacuated — the date was 4th June late in the day.

Suddenly there was a slight movement and the first enemy soldier was belly gliding cautiously onto the beach. He raised his rifle and sighted, and with gentle pressure on the trigger the bullet took the German neatly between the eyes. He was killed instantly.

Almost immediately hundreds of green clad figures were milling onto the beach looking round for the enemy. They found him, as his remaining bullets cut them down. They dropped flat into the sand and sent murderous bursts of fire towards him and when their fire was not returned they knew they had him. A German Officer gave a gutteral command as he strode towards this English Soldier who was now standing proudly before them. His Luger raised, he advanced nearer and they were all very bewildered when the Englishman suddenly turned his back on them and faced the sea . . . He quickly stripped his rifle down in a last gesture of defiance — magazine — bolt — and quickly threw them one after the other in different directions far out to sea. "The sods will not have them," he thought.

Angrily the German Officer menacingly said "Tommy Come". Tommy went.... He knew without fear of contradiction that come what may, England would win the final Battle.

The smoke from the burning Oil Tanks drifted heavily across the beach . . . DUNKIRK HAD FALLEN.

In 1970 the Commemorative Medal of Dunkirk instituted after the war by the Town of Dunkirk for those of the French Forces who served in the Dunkirk area was made available to the British who fought in the same arena in 1940.

It's a medal all Veterans wear with pride but at the same time sadness because the British Government fail to give due recognition. Until 'The Miracle' is recognised I'm afraid the Veterans must continue to receive the same answer to their many applications for a medal award — "no further awards can be instituted for the 1939-45 war."

In these days when the pulpits of the land are silent about the miracles of the Bible, even explaining them away and reducing Jesus Christ to a mere man. We should not be too surprised that the only things people believe in are selfishness, greed, adultery, lying etc. We should not be too surprised when anarchy raises its ugly head and evil men design the downfall of the nation. Against such a background what hope have the Veterans in their quest for a British Medal?

For all time Dunkirk will remain in their hearts, for who can forget a Miracle. Of all medals displayed this is the one they long to wear on that especially reserved left side of the chest. A custom dating back to the 11th century when the Christian Crusaders wore their emblem, a cross on the left side of their attire near the heart. This badge received protection by the shield, also bearing a cross and carried by the left arm. Whilst the right arm wielded the sword.

The issue of a medal would provide Britons with a needy reminder that for nearly a thousand years we have not successfully been invaded. It would cause to be written into the page of modern British history with fresh ink of an hour when the nation low in morale, enshrouded in impenetrable gloom, engaged in conflict between light and darkness, good and evil received the protecting shield of God. Providing valuable time for the right arm of combat to be strengthened and ultimately destroy Hitler's Germany. It would tell the British youth that freedom is precious; that the Miracle of Dunkirk is the hinge upon which the door opened for the Keeping of Britain and the World.

Nationally and individually the British People believe in God. At the present moment in time such belief is deeply buried and needs arousing. I believe that a delay does not always indicate a denial. More often than not timing has to be right for the fulfilment of desire.

After the defeat of the Armada — due almost entirely to weather conditions — Queen Elizabeth I recognised this. She had a medal struck which bore the inscription 'He blew with His winds and they were scattered.' How wonderful it would be if Queen Elizabeth II could follow it up with a medal inscribed 'Thou hast given a great deliverance.'

I am right behind every Veteran in their determination for recognition but it would appear H. M. Government intend a continuance of refusal in their generalised statement of no further awards for the 1939-45 war. Whilst this, according to officialdom cannot be interpreted as a 'personal' rebuff, nevertheless Dunkirk Veterans feel like forgotten men.

Perhaps they need to consider a fresh approach to the whole matter, bearing in mind that the oft utilised term, 'Dunkirk Spirit' is applicable to the whole nation. In these days of diminishing values, the collapse of standards and the breath of ungodliness which pervades, I believe it would be a shot in the arm of the nation to remind itself of one 20th century 'Miracle' if the Royal Mint struck a Commemorative Crown for general circulation throughout the British Isles, depicting the "Miracle of Deliverance'. Not only in Britain but throughout the Commonwealth and the World people will own a lasting memorial to the 1940 epic causing fresh enquiry to what it is all about? Britain has a message to give the world of tottering thrones, dictators and unstable republics. But firstly Britons themselves must re-capture the Spirit of Dunkirk by becoming once again a God fearing people.

Together with a set of Commemorative Postage Stamps I feel sure the soldiers, sailors and airmen plus those who prayed, worked and lived to save Britain from captivity would find within themselves a stirring of Faith resulting in a sorely needed resurrection of British Spirit — a rebirth of the 'Dunkirk Spirit' touching the lives of this materialistic generation. Then and only then will Dunkirk Veterans feel satisfied for although daily death reduces their ranks they have sure knowledge that new warriors of the self-same calibre take their place.

GLORY AND GRACE

I preached of Jesus, how He died for men.
I desired that some one would shout 'Amen!'
There came one to me who said, 'Is that so?'
'But that thing happened a long time ago!'

111

There are many who do not seem to care,
They have no interest at all in Prayer.
Yet without sound of the beating of drums
The moment that I pray God's answer comes.

And I do what God the Father decrees
Thus I live in a condition of ease.
Helpless and orphaned souls indeed are they
Who live without God, and in their own way.

Christ and I together can face anything,
Friendship with Him is good for soul making.
My soul cleansed from sin, my life sanctified,
Is possible because for *me* Jesus died.

He from a character such as mine
Has caused the light of His glory to shine
My redeemed nature is shown in my face
For I am the recipient of great grace.
              VETERAN EDDIE FOULKES, D.C.M., M.M., C de G.
                                              MANCHESTER

IF

If you can make a promise, and by that promise stand,
If you can take a beating and then shake the victor's hand,
If you can do a deed without looking for the glory,
If you can hold your tongue when you hear a gossip's story,
If you can make good better, and try to make bad good,
If you can keep your soul alive with the Grace of God as food,
If you can carry on until life's craggy road should end,
Then here's my hand, my comrade, you've made a life-long
friend.

                    VETERAN HARRY CORBIERE
                    GRIMSBY

112

The British Memorial, Dunkirk, on the road to Furnes — unveiled by Her Majesty The Queen Mother 1958.

EPILOGUE

Whither Bound?

In 1940 Britain stood alone, engaged in a conflict for the right to remain a free people. The nine days of Dunkirk ensured that freedom from Hitlerism and enslavement.

Today, Britain faces new enemies in a world threatened by global war, the climate seasoned by a world riven by the menace of anarchy with so called 'liberation' movements for this and that fostering any iniquitous cause aimed at human corruption, loss of life and general disruption. Indeed, the whole force of the current tribulation is directed to the end that all things may be shaken. We live in the age of the terrorist, the mugger, the rapist. Britain's Saturday afternoon at the soccer match constantly receives attention from the news media as hooliganism on the terraces creates fearful scenes. Even on the pitch highly paid players lose control of themselves giving way to thuggery and argument. Voices here and there condemn but offer little in the way of solution. When human nature comes under the microscope it is so easy to submit negative criticism which does nothing more than thicken the gloom.

In 1966, as if by prophetic insight, I foresaw much of what we have on the soccer scene. But who really wanted to listen? Under the headline 'Parson And The Soccer Toughs', the Daily Mirror quoted me thus: "There is an answer to unfriendly mannerisms on the field, in the form of a change in human nature." I wrote to many leading clubs offering them a united service in Grimsby's Town Hall or London's Royal Albert Hall when I would deal with the cause of 'uncontrol' and provide the answer to 'perfect discipline'. One manager upon being approached by the press retorted: "With me and the players, football is something of a religion." What a silly answer! Is it any wonder we now have a Saturday reign of madness?

The foregoing illustration serves to underline that in all our national ills we are confronted by two mental enemies: complacency and defeatism. If in 1940 such characteristics had been permitted to rule, I wonder what sort of regime we would now be under?

These two evil anaesthetics drug the people as the whole fabric of society is fragmenting. Many seem lulled to the extent of putting up with whatever preposterous evil comes their way; paral-

114

ised and afraid to face it in the way their fathers would have done. The revealing truth is that we have forgotten the God who showed Himself in Jesus Christ — we have forgotten the Divine Hand that has preserved, protected and led this nation — we have forgotten Dunkirk — A Miracle of Deliverance. Because of this the Veterans are fighting a losing battle in their quest to receive some form of recognition. When the people get back to God — then and only then will the Dunkirk epic be seen in its true colours. Typical of the prevalent attitude is the letter received from the Post Office H.Q., in response to my request to the Prime Minister for a set of postage stamps to commemorate the Dunkirk Deliverance:

> The Post Office policy in regard to the issue of special stamps is that they shall conform with the following criteria:—
>
> 1. To celebrate events of national and international importance.
> 2. To commemorate important anniversaries in multiples of 50 years (exceptionally 25 years for Royal occasions).
> 3. To reflect the British contribution to world affairs including the arts and sciences.
> 4. To extend public patronage to the arts by encouraging the development of minuscule art.
>
> I regret therefore, that as your suggestion does not conform with the criteria, we cannot consider the subject for a special stamp issue.

In addition I suggested that the Royal Mint strike a special commemorative crown. They replied:

> Issues of commemorative pieces in the British coinage have been very infrequent and invariably timed to coincide with a specific event or with its commonly celebrated anniversary (ie. 25th, 50th, etc.) While there may be no doubt that the National Day of prayer on 26th May, 1940 was a notable event in our history, the idea of commemorating it by the issue of a special coin therefore seems unlikely to command sufficient support at the present time.

I'm sure the Veterans will be delighted to learn that according to the Post Office their 'deliverance' was not of National importance. The Royal Mint's statement, 'unlikely to command sufficient support at the present time', brings us to the heart of affairs and the sad conclusion that inexorably, the Christian religion which for centuries has shaped and formed the character of our people is fast disappearing from our national life. During the office of Prime Minister Harold Wilson, I asked him to consider calling a National Day of Prayer. He replied

> . . . while your anxiety for Her Majesty the Queen to call a

115

National Day of Prayer is understood and appreciated, Mr. Wilson has decided that he ought not to make a recommendation in the sense at the moment.

In the past, National Days of Prayer have always been reserved for special occasions which are of the very gravest moment, and it is from this they have derived their peculiar force and value.

Meanwhile, a hurricane of evil smites the nation, removing the landmarks carefully laid by Britons of incomparable tenacity. The feckless unable to match the rancorous creed of those bent upon destroying our way of life that our people no longer dwell in freedom and safety. These agents of anarchy and irreligion infiltrate every strata of society and things are now so bad that any Christian worth his salt is hard beset to preserve a stand for what is right.

My church is located on Grimsby's newest housing estate. Naturally it is not without its problems. A few years ago, the Rent and Ratepayers Association called a public meeting with the express purpose of launching a rent strike. A leaflet posted through my letter box, grubby in appearance and deadly insofar as content, made up my mind to be at the meeting.

The chairman wasted no time in introducing the six willing tenants who had been duped into the 'guinea pig' role of agreeing to say "me no pay", next time the rent man called. Warlike speeches resounded from the floor and it appeared to me that the main provocateurs had nothing to do with the estate or even lived in the town. Everything was 'cut and dried', ready for implementation when I stood to my feet asking for permission to speak. The Grimsby Evening Telegraph Municipal Correspondent reported:

Militant Tenants on Grimsby's Willows Estate last night backed a rent strike call — despite a passionate appeal from a clergyman not to sow the seeds of anarchy in the town. . . .
The lone voice raised in protest against the meeting's decision was that of the Rev. Frederick Grossmith, minister of the Calvary Church. He objected strongly to the rent strike and to the wording of leaflets distributed throughout the big estate publicising the meeting. Mr. Grossmith told the meeting that phrases in the leaflet telling tenants they could not rely on 'sell out councils' and urging them to 'stand and fight' by withholding the amount of the increases 'looks like anarchy to me'. The minister added 'I want to speak on the moral and Christian issues imposed by a rent strike.
'I would urge you to reconsider as individuals the method of protest and ask you to utilise legal and proven methods. I think to use illegal methods is to sow the seeds of anarchy. There are people within our society who are preparing for revolution and who want to bring the country to a standstill,

116

and I think there is a serious moral issue here.
'Let us not contribute to the dishonesty of this country nowadays', he added. . . .

After the meeting, a group surrounded me showing on their faces the hostility they felt inside. Much I had said they twisted, adding insult and derision. With difficulty I managed to leave the meeting place. Before I reached home my wife had received an anonymous telephone call which threatened my safe being. Before the end of that week, thousands of leaflets had been handed out on the estate and in the town's main shopping centre headed: 'REV. GROSSMITH'S REMARKS ANGER HUMBERSIDE WORKERS'. The leaflet relegated me to the ranks of a 'nut case' and an 'ogre'. A number of shop windows carried posters to similar effect and even at the begging of several town councillors they would not take them down. I have been 'pilloried' for a just crusade and exercising my right to express just what I felt. Herein lies the difference; even though I may not agree with a man, I would defend with my life his right to expression.

I believe that when God comes first in your life and you do what is right in His eyes, according to the promises of the Bible, God honours His servants. Happily, the strike never took place, which saved the Grimsby Council many thousands of pounds. And possibly a lot of people bringing upon themselves a situation they would later regret. Something else happened which will remain with me all my days. At the meeting in question I clashed with a very prominent union leader. However, in honesty I must say that this particular man maintained dignity and unknown to himself was used by the agitators. Some months later this man called me to his home. Upon arrival I found him and his wife in much distress. Their 34-year old son lay in the hospital rapidly departing this life and I was asked to visit him. When I arrived at the hospital I knew I was calling upon someone not expected to live more than three or four days. After speaking and praying with the man I left a copy of 'The Living Bible' an easily readable modern translation. A week later I revisited; although very weak and frail and in much discomfort he turned to me and said: 'have you come for your book?' I replied: 'No! It's yours to keep.' With a tear in his eye, his voice almost a whisper he smiled: 'I've nearly finished it.'

I was quite taken back and upon enquiry learned that he had given instructions for his television and hobby books to be removed so that he could finish reading the Bible. "Has the message of the Bible gotten inside of you?" I asked. "Funny you say that. I was part way through when just like a key going into the lock something unlocked inside of me and I feel so different now." Ronald now knew the meaning of life having made his peace with God by receiving Jesus Christ as His Lord and Saviour. He lived another couple of days on God's extended time; sufficient enough to finish off the last chapters of the Bible. Upon telling his father the story, immediately he jumped up and telephoned the hospital with instructions that The Bible must be returned with his son's possession. Ronald's baby daughter, when old enough would be given her father's Bible and told how the God of the Bible became real to him.

Sir Arthur Bryant said: "A nation which forgets its past has no future." Where then are we heading? Whither Bound? In 1940 a common enemy drew us together in prayer and dedication. Now another enemy jeopardises the very destiny of our national existence: sowing the ugly seeds of chaos and disorder with the tragic harvest of a discontented, disenchanted, frustrated, benumbed people. The pressure of evil is so convincing and so widespread there remains one single avenue of hope. Firstly, judgement must begin at the House of God — away with the pale, palsied preaching which removes the 'miracle' element of Christianity and back to the God of the Bible. The nation stands in peril, as disobedient and lost as the Children of Israel in their wilderness wanderings. Why? Because like John Bunyan's 'Pilgrim', we have lost 'our role'. When the authority of the Bible is 'lost', the people lose sight of a covenant keeping God. How we need to pray, 'Turn us again, O God of hosts, and cause they face to shine, and we shall be saved', Psalm 80 v. 7.

In this hour of need and unprecedented grief, what better news could the nation receive than, 'The Lord is their inheritance'. But people ask, 'Who is the Lord?' There is a growing consciousness that revival must come otherwise we are doomed. A revival is a period of religious awakening; it is a time of harvest; it is history repeating itself and ordinary people standing where our forefathers stood. By revelation discovering first hand that Jesus Christ truly is who he claimed to be. Non other than God in the flesh — the Saviour. Unless a revival takes place, soon we are going to enter a period of precariousness, calamity and disaster. The Bible says: "Righteousness exalteth a nation but sin is a reproach to any people'. Britain's sins ascend up as a stench in the nostrils of God. The people have raised up new gods and images which receive their worship and dedication. We are either going to have a revival of God's ways or experience a punishment more sore and terrible than ever experienced.

Of all our institutions, the Crown is a symbol of unity. At her Coronation our Queen was given the Kingly sword and bidden by the Archbishop of Canterbury in God's name to "do justice, stop the growth of iniquity, protect the Holy Church of God . . . restore the things that are gone to decay. . ." Although it is constitutional for Her Majesty to be guided by the advice of responsible Ministers, it is the duty of such Ministers to remember that Her Majesty is Head of both Church and State. The personal influence of the Crown is of sacred consequence, and daily we should unite in praying that all blockades to its free expression shall be removed.

Before it's too late, I pray we shall arise from the sleep of death. We shall remember the past and take heart and encouragement. Now is the time to 'restore the things that are gone to decay'. May our Queen, like her late father and grandfather be guided to express a desire to call this nation to a 'Day of Prayer and Repentance'. Are we to await the total destruction, dismantling and demoralisation of the land, providing a prepared stage for men of evil intent to take over, before we realise that our continuance as a nation depends upon nurturing a living peremptory contact with the Throne of God?

It is reported that when Hitler walked into Warsaw he wept, not because he felt remorse at the sight of the terrible destruction and suffering inflicted but because it spoilt the effect of his triumphal entry. In consequence, he ordered Nazi airmen to concentrate their bombing only on the suburbs of Paris. Preserving at all cost the heart of the city. Surely then his constant bombardment of London indicated he had abandoned all hope of ever entering this capital city as a conqueror? In 1940, the alarm was sounded and Britons found like the Psalmist of old that 'mine help cometh from the Lord'. Hitler's aspirations disintegrated for prayer has the effect of concentrating our energies and opening up our hearts to the power of spiritual forces. That same power can be released again to swat like flies the enemies which now threaten.

After Dunkirk men of high rank and position in the land recognised the continued necessity of Divine Aid. Major Wellesley Tudor-Pole and Colonel W.H. Carver, M.P., hit upon a tremendous idea for uniting the nation. As a point of contact they chose the chimes of Big Ben and urged people at 8.59 p.m. each night as they prepared to listen to the 9 o'clock news on the radio to observe a one minute silence. It was to be a rallying point for the personal renewal of courage, determination and faith. This Dedicated Moment was shared by millions throughout the land, at sea and even in occupied territories. The King, Prime Minister and Ecclesiastical leaders gave it their wholehearted support. Sir Waldron Smithers, M.P. — Chairman of the Big Ben Silent Minute Observance Council said:

> No more effective way can be found than by uniting each evening at 9 o'clock. In unity is strength. This universal wrestling match is between good and evil, between the Cross and the swastika. Let us come together each evening.

The present upheaval leaves a question mark ... Whither Bound? The confrontation of vast powers of evil working against our beloved land must be met. It is worse than presumption on our part to attempt to counter such evil in our own strength. May the Dunkirk Spirit baptise us afresh; for I like to think of Britain at that time as standing in the same plight as Israel's tribe of Gad, of whom we read in Genesis 49:19 "A troop shall overcome him; but he shall overcome at the last."

For a while Hitler's might came upon us like a troop. And for a moment they overcame us; it was painful and we should have succumbed if we had not by faith approached the Throne of God. A war is not evaluated by its first successes or defeats, but by that which happens 'at the last'. I pray in these critical and crucial days that as in 1940 we shall . . . arise! . . . meet the challenge . . . and like Gad . . . 'OVERCOME AT THE LAST'.